living DANDE

A Green Cookbook

Deborah Richmond

Living Dande

Order this book online at www.trafford.com
or email orders@trafford.com

Most Trafford titles are also available at major online book retailers.

© Copyright 2012 Deborah Richmond.

All rights reserved. No part of this publication may be reproduced, stored in a retrieval system, or transmitted, in any form or by any means, electronic, mechanical, photocopying, recording, or otherwise, without the written prior permission of the author.

Printed in the United States of America.

ISBN: 978-1-4251-2754-1 (sc)

Trafford rev. 04/28/2012

 www.trafford.com

North America & international
toll-free: 1 888 232 4444 (USA & Canada)
phone: 250 383 6864 ♦ fax: 812 355 4082

May you always live dande!
Your friend, Deborah Richmond

Living Dande

A GREEN COOKBOOK

By Debbie Richmond

Disclaimer

This web site/book (www.livingdande.com, www.greencookbook.ca) and its recommendations are not designed to replace a professional medical diagnosis and treatment. It is the sole intent of the owner/author to offer knowledge of a general nature and to create an understanding.

Please note: Dandelion greens are now available, year round in some grocery stores, seasonally in health food stores and local markets. If you start to look around you might find some growing in your own garden or your friends, backyard. You can substitute dandelions for spinach greens, in these green cookbook recipes. Just remember, green is good, but dandelions are for Living Dande.

Stay healthy. Stay green.

By: Debbie Richmond

Table of Contents

Acknowledgments	7
Letter of Appreciation from George Smitherman, Ontario, Canada, Minister of Health & Long Term Care	8
Dandelion Nutrition: Living Dande Matters	9
"Living Dande" Rhyme by Deborah L. Richmond	12
Introduction	13
Looking Back: A History	15
Appetizers made with Dandegreens	17
Dandegreen and Egg Dishes	37
Dandegreens in Pasta	57
Dandegreen Salads	75
Dandegreen Soups	131
Dandegreen Smoothies	149
Dandegreen Vegetable side dishes	155
Dandegreen Main Course Meals	181
Dandelion Teasers	227
Cancer Story by George Cairns	241
Other testimony	246
Metric Equivalents	249
Children's Story	251
About the Author	253
My Vision	255

Acknowledgements

    I'd like to thank my family and friends for supporting me while on my journey to collect, consume, share information and study dandelions. Special thanks to those who typed endlessly recipe after recipe, those who shared their knowledge, or encouraged me, and to those that donated information and recipes to my cause. I'm very grateful.

    This collection of stories and recipes and has taken me many years to compile, perfect and indeed find my own joy. I sure hope this green cookbook helps you feel the joy, dandelion health brings.

    Make and share a dandelion dish today, and start your own healing process.

Deborah Jaynes-Richmond

Ministry of Health and Long-Term Care

Office of the Deputy Premier

10th Floor, Hepburn Block
80 Grosvenor Street
Toronto ON M7A 2C4
Tel 416-327-4300
Fax 416-326-1571
www.health.gov.on.ca

Ministère de la Santé et des Soins de longue durée

Bureau du vice-premier ministre

10e étage, édifice Hepburn
80, rue Grosvenor
Toronto ON M7A 2C4
Tél 416-327-4300
Téléc 416-326-1571
www.health.gov.on.ca

Ontario

November 3, 2007

Dear Rebaah,

Just a brief note to say what a pleasure it was to meet you recently.

Thanks for your contribution to the health of Ontarians.

Warmly,

George

George Smitherman
Minister of Health
& Long-term care
Ontario

Dandelion Nutrition: Living Dande Matters

One of our oldest known plants is the dandelion. Earliest finds of dandelions date back as far as thirty million years. Originally from Eurasia, settlers migrated to other continents and brought them along. Still highly regarded for use by many cultures, for all too many people the dandelion has become a pesky weed. A shame really, that this plant has become of such ill repute in the minds of so many.

The dandelion is really a magnificent plant, medicinal healing herb, and a healthy source of edible food. Its Latin name, " Taraxacum Official" means the "Official Remedy for Disorders." Its French name "Dent-de-lion" translates to lions tooth. This refers to its jagged, 3" to 10" green leaves. Its yellow rosette flowers are 1" to 2" inches in diameter, held up by a hollow stem. The edible flowers and green leaves are used in recipes, fresh or cooked, and also in wine. The white sap that oozes from the central taproot is said to eliminate warts when applied repeatedly to the affected areas. I was told that during World War II the sap was gathered to make latex rubber products such as rubber gloves.

The root is the most potent medicinal part of the plant. The soil also benefits from this plant releasing nourishing nitrogen and minerals back into the ground. Dandelions are rich in vitamins and minerals (the essential building blocks of life) and benefit our organs and functions. The dandelion flower heads are the first to attract the bees and share their sweet nectar to be turned into honey. Then, once withered, the heads soon turn to seed carried by tiny parachute-like marvels. The wind carries them afar and helps them re-seed and spread. If eaten, the seeds are said to have antifungal properties.

The raw green dandelion leaves contain only 45 kcal per 100 grams, 2.7 grams of vegetable protein, and 9.2 grams of carbohydrates. No wonder that this has been a desired ingredient in Mediterranean and Middle Eastern cooking! The nutrients and minerals found in the dandelion show "0" cholesterol and, if eaten daily, provide much of our sustainable nutrition. A serving of dandelions provides 24% of our daily requirement of iron, 19% of calcium, 23% of vitamin E, 16% manganese, and a long list of B-vitamins. Its highest mineral concentration is in vitamin C at 42%, beta carotene at 54%, and vitamin A at 64%. Vitamin K comes in at a whopping 74%. Adding salt or cooking our dandelions, the mineral levels drop somewhat from the raw amounts mentioned above, but are still worthy of note and benefit to the digestion.

Dandelions show analgesic (pain killing) properties, are anti-allergenic and anti- carcinogenic agents, have anti-fungal and anti – fibrotic properties. Dandelions are said to increase libido (sex drive), and lower blood sugar in diabetics. Dandelions are a digestive aid that stimulates the growth of enzymes and 14 strains of bifida bacteria. Then there are its therapeutic effects against the development of colitis, diarrhea, cancerous tumors, or kidney and bladder stones. Dandelions protect against chemically induced injury. In short, their high boost of minerals and vitamins simply makes the body just want to run better.

The dandelion really is a spectacular plant with much hidden goodness. Eating dandelions for food is something the body understands. Dandelions make for easy food to provide. We need to eat like nature intended us to eat: gather and hunt. Dandelions are living plants. No need to poison them and along the way poison our property. It is easy to pull them up and eat them instead. Not to mention that the toxins will not stay in one spot and may well come back to haunt soil and water supply. Food bears a direct influence on our body's ability to absorb and use minerals and nutrients.

It feels good to detoxify the body's system and prevent inflammation causing high tissue acidity, a condition that over half of the world's population suffers from. An acidic pH level in our body opens the door to gastro-intestinal conditions relating to bloating, gas, diarrhea, constipation, metabolic diseases, diabetes, fibromyalgia, depression, confusion, anxiety, and cancer. Unwanted acidity also affects adrenal and hormone levels and maybe even auto-immune reactions. Dandelions offer beneficial antioxidant action and tissue regeneration by reducing free radicals.

Think green means clean: The transition to greening the body with this environmentally friendly plant, makes un-wellness disappear. It is easy to start enjoying this lowly food from the Gods today. Good luck searching for your dandelions. So you too can feel fine and dandy, by following the recipes in "My Green Cookbook," you too will be "Living Dande."

Think Green, Think Environmentally Green!

Ode to the Dandelion

I want you to know that the universe planned to sow, these dandelions that grow, green at toe. History says so, we're supposed to know, it helps toxins flow, out of your bowels and kidneys they go. All your organs, even your bones, now your eyes are much better, I'm thankful and don't I know it. Oh, something that is still free, oh, it has to be, it makes your body run better, you can pick them in almost any weather. It's time to come together. At markets, in gardens, get your dandelions daily, for optimal impaction on your systems. Some say let us be sick, overweight or let the people around the world starve, because they weren't given the seed to sow yet. Oh, I hope I can bridge the gap. Others are invited to join in and help keep wellness on tap.

Original poem by Debbie Richmond

PSALM 65: 11, 12. "You'll crown the year with your goodness, and your paths drip with abundance. They drop on the pastures of the wilderness, and the little hills rejoice on every side."

"Living Dande"

I don't want to get old and hurtful.
I've hurt enough. I found "Joy", while I had things rough.
My journey may help others now. If I get the word out, learning to "know how" shouldn't be so tough.
If you treat yourself with respect, often others will too. If I get the word out, you'll know what to do!
You can get some dandelions; things will start to turn about. Your body, it's your temple, just try some and find out.
This message is very simple, Nature works in harmony to compliment your wellness
It's detoxifying, it's free!
Our overall Healthcare could be less taxed our grocery bills cheaper because you can use the whole plant.
Leaf or seed, flower or root, a great boost of nutrients that gives pain the boot. It's a diuretic you know, so just watch your inflammation go.
Sow the seeds I say, and if given away, could help keep someone's hunger away.
In any country, anywhere, these lessons learned, may make disease disappear.
If an earthy cup of tea is what you'd like my dear, I think it's time you tried some, and watch your depression disappear.
So I guess that's all I have to say, it all could be summed up this way.
Try some from your yard today, if you have kept the chemicals away.
Please enjoy these recipes, and remember if you can't find dandelions, substitute spinach or other greens you find, you'll feel awesome.
Green is good!

Original poem by Debbie Richmond

Introduction

I remember many days and holiday gatherings with my family questioning my Grandmother with intense curiosity on her lifestyle and what she fed her family, how she prepared the food and how she preserved the food for the winter months. After losing her husband suddenly, soon after her sixth child was born, my Grandmother was forced to become the sole bread winner and care giver to her children. It was during the 1930's and 1940's. It wasn't so much as being a bread winner back then but, rather the sole provider for food, clothing and shelter. Looking to the land was the only answer. There were no grocery stores to go browsing and down the aisles. There was no 9 to 5 job and no paycheck at the end of the week.

The local general store sold flour and sugar which they could buy if they sold enough eggs or if there was an extra calf to sell. My Grandmother taught her children how to live off the land. So vegetables, bread, milk, meat on occasion, homemade cheese from the few milking cows, apples and berries when they came into season were the foods they grew with. Life was hard, work was never ending, cold nights, no new shoes, home sewn clothes. Some people say life was simpler.... Was it really? There are times when I wish I could turn back the clock and live like my Granny, but only in a time capsule. My little Granny lived to be 103 and danced at her 100th birthday party with her 102 year old brother, whom eventually lived to be 105. Thank you for the memories...

Passing on our traditions to our children is very important. Learning how to prepare natural whole clean foods should be fundamental. Going back to our ROOTS should never be forgotten. We can learn from our ancestors, even if it is only one or two generations back.

It is unlikely that I will preserve my eggs in a bucket filled with rock salt, but if I had too, I could.

Did our ancestors really know the health benefits from their foods that grew wild in the fields? Do you really think it was a fluke that the Dandelion Greens and roots became a tonic for them? Of course not...... If you study symptomatology, the causes and cures you will learn by health variations that we and, our ancestors knew only too well their own body functions adapted well with dandelions whether it be the roots or leaves. Historical and modern day Master Herbalists from around the world have reported health benefits from the simple addition of this little ragged leaf plant. There are hundreds of documented cases.

This book is filled with our ancestor's collections. Tried and tested over generations. Some of the recipes have been adapted for our modern times. There are also some new and inventive ways to prepare this block buster plant and incorporate them into your diet.

I find it very unusual why we don't find this bright yellow spectacular flower, which brightens our day in spring--a welcome to bring in the new season. It's a time for cleansing and renewing after the long winter. Warm detoxifying c of dandelion tea, dandelion salad greens, roasted dandelion roots which taste like mild coffee and of course those bright yellow flowers which can carpet our fields make a wonderful sweet wine. Oh yes…. I can remember gathering flower tops with my family in bags so my parents could make wine. I was too young to enjoy it then, but "oh my" the lessons we have learnt. I can't wait for spring……..

Shelley Atchison-Brown
RNOP, NAET, NHC
Live Cell Analyst
Educational Director-International Academy of Advanced Nutrition

10 Dandelion leaves a day for 2 weeks is supposed to bring joy. That mind body connection.

Looking Back: A History

In the 1920's, a clinic opened using dandelions in South Western Ontario Canada, doctors were sending their most ill patients here. Their good success was made, until government and officials, alike, caused so much red tape, that it forced them to close their doors.

As told by Debbie Richmond by her friend;
Dietrich Newmann (Nutritionist)

What does this tell you? Sometimes you just have to take what nature gives you that makes sense and use it.

Please don't think of them as offensive but for what they truly are as herbs, medicinal, natural, nutritional prescription from the earth, for our good health that is perfectly safe to put in our mouths. They may become your "saving grace", like it has been for me.

My next door neighbor was using a dandelion digger to clean her yard of a few. I asked her to save the dandelions for me, half a garbage bag later, I got my wish. A couple of hours of cleaning, I now had 4 cups of dandelion root. I chop and slightly warm dry for use in tea, but you will see many other uses for the whole plant throughout this book. Ask your neighbors for dandelions. Hey!! Start a small business to supply stores, markets or clinic. I guess I'm saying to make good use of the dandelions given to us. Try a recipe from my green cookbook today!!! Your body will be glad you did.

Appetizers made with Dandegreens

*Are dandelions so bad that they need poisoning?
No! The fact that they are abundant just means that there is a lot of nourishment for us. (M. Walton)*

Individual Dandelion Quiches

Pastry for 2 pie crusts
2 tbsp. olive oil
10 oz. of dandelion greens, chopped
¼ lb. cheese of choice, shredded
1 cup half-and-half cream
3 eggs
1 tsp. sea salt
⅛ tsp. pepper

Grease and flour 36 muffin pan cups, then prepare pastry. On lightly floured surface, roll dough about ⅛ inch thick. Using cookie cutter, cut dough into 36 circles. Line muffin pan cups with pastry circles. Brush pastry lightly with olive oil. Chill 30 minutes. Drain dandelion greens on paper towel. Into each cup, spoon about 1 tsp. dandelion and top with some cheese. Wisk together in a small bowl half-and-half cream, eggs, sea salt and pepper, spoon about 1 tbsp. egg mixture into each cup. Bake 25 minutes or until knife inserted in center comes out clean. Remove from pan and serve. Enjoy with sliced tomatoes on the side.

Green is good. Rediscover the Dandelion wisdom.

Salmon Dip

1 cup herbed or plain cream cheese
1 cup of dandelion greens, washed and chopped
1 lb. salmon cooked and cooled
1 tsp. lemon juice
1 tsp. soy sauce
3 tbsp. minced onion
½ tsp. dill dried
½ tsp. Cayenne pepper to taste
Sea salt and pepper to taste

Puree all of the ingredients in blender until smooth
Place in serving dish.
Cover and chill for 2 hrs.
Enjoy this dip with sliced vegetables, rice crisps or crackers.

Dandelions are more than just a meal; it's a reminder of a way of life, not seen in this country in generations. It recalls a time when Mother Nature dictated what you were going to do for the day. How you would dress and what you were going to eat etc.

Dandelion & Feta in Phyllo with Mushrooms

1 cup chopped dandelion greens, per person
½ cup chopped mushrooms, per person
¼ cup crumbled feta cheese per person
2 sheets phyllo pastry per person
2 tbsp. olive oil
Sea salt and pepper to taste

Mix dandelion greens, feta cheese, mushrooms, sea salt and pepper well in small bowl. Set aside.
Lay the 2 sheets of phyllo on top of each other and brush with olive oil. Spread dandelion mixture on the phyllo pastry, and roll like a log.
Brush with olive oil, slice in ¼ to ½ inch, lay on a cookie sheet, and bake at 350°F for 20 minutes, until pastry is golden brown.
Enjoy these tasty pastries alone, as an appetizer, or on the side at lunch or dinner.

Dandelion Information Lost to the Public.
-It's known for its cleaning job on our insides.
-Teachers should share dandelion wisdom with students

Dandelion Ranch Dip

¾ cup sour cream or low fat yogurt
½ cup ranch dressing
7 - 8 cups cut dandelions
½ cup finally shredded carrots
½ cup finally chopped yellow pepper

Mix sour cream and dressing in medium bowl until well blended.
Add remaining ingredients; mix well. Cover.
Refrigerate at least 1 hour before serving.
Serve with your favorite vegetables. Enjoy.

Change your life style to "Dandelions", and help your whole body feel better.

Dandelion Oysters Rockefeller

36 large oysters in shell
2 to 3 cups chopped dandelion greens
2 tbsp. olive oil
1 tbsp. minced onion
3 tbsp. minced fresh parsley
½ tsp. sea salt
1 tbsp. Worcestershire sauce
¼ tsp. cayenne pepper, or to your taste preference
1 cup light cream
Parmesan cheese (optional)

Carefully remove oysters from shells. Set aside. Select 36 shell halves; those that will sit level are best. Rinse well. Place open side up, in two 12x7x2 inch oven proof casseroles. Microwave covered, on HI, (max power) 8 to 9 minutes. Drain well. Place oysters between paper towels and squeeze dry. Mix dandelion, olive oil, onion, parsley, sea salt, Worcestershire, cayenne pepper, and cream. Spoon shell half full of the dandelion mixture and place an oyster in the middle and sprinkle generously with Parmesan cheese. Cover each baking dish with foil. Place both dishes on middle rack of oven. Cook on 370°F 15 to 20 minutes, or until oysters are plump and edges curled. Let stand 5 minutes before serving. Garnish with lemon wedges.
Enjoy.

I see the Old Ways and the New Ways in Balance.

Dandelion Dip

8 oz. light cream cheese, softened
½ cup low fat yogurt
2 tsp. lemon juice
½ tsp. sea salt
½ tsp. Worcestershire sauce
⅛ tsp. garlic powder
½ cup chopped green onion
3 cups chopped dandelion greens

Mash first 7 ingredients together with fork in bowl.
Add dandelion. Stir. Turn into slow cooker. Cover.
Cook on low for 1 and 1\2 hours, stirring every 30 minutes, until warm.
Serve with favorite vegetables and/or pumpernickel bread pieces.

-

The importance of internal cleansing is for optimal wellness.

Baked Dandelion Dip Loaf

2 (8 oz. each) cream cheese, softened
1 cup low fat yogurt
3 cups dandelion greens, dried
1 cup shredded cheddar cheese
8 oz. can water chestnuts, drained and chopped
5 slices pershuto bacon or ham
1 green onion, chopped
2 tsp. dill weed
1 garlic clove, minced
½ tsp. sea salt
⅛ tsp. pepper
1 unsliced round loaf sourdough or pumpernickel bread
 Raw vegetables

In mixing bowl, beat cream cheese and low fat yogurt. Stir in next nine ingredients. Cut top of bread; set aside. Hollow out bottom leaving a ½ inch shell. Cube removed bread and set aside. Fill shell with dandelion dip; replace top, wrap in tin foil and put on baking sheet Bake in 375°F oven for 1 ¼ hours or until dip is heated through. Open tin foil. Serve warm with bread and vegetables.

I'm mixing a personal experience with something creative. It's like eating dandelions a whole new way.

Pumpernickel Bread Dip

5 - 6 cups dandelion leaves
Wash and scissor cut to smaller pieces
Microwave until limp (seconds)
Squeeze out all the moisture.
1 cup low fat yogurt
1 cup of sour cream
2 green onions chopped
2 drops of Worcestershire sauce
1 pkg. of dry vegetable soup mix
1 tsp. of lemon juice
Water chestnuts optional

Mix all ingredients together. Cut the top of the pumpernickel bread in a circular fashion. Lift the interior of the bread out to replace with your dip. Take the bread that you just cut and break into bite size pieces for dipping. Enjoy!

You should be accountable for everything you eat. Kind of like when you use a credit card.

Dandelion Pâté

8 cups chopped dandelion greens
¼ cup olive oil
1 cup thinly sliced green onions
2 large carrots, coarsely shredded
1 cup half-and-half cream
1 ¾ tsp. sea salt
1 tsp. basil
⅛ tsp. cayenne pepper or to personal taste
4 eggs

Place dandelion in colander in sink; using back of wooden spoon, press dandelion to remove moisture. With knife or scissors, finely chop dandelion.
Grease loaf pan and line bottom with foil. In saucepan over medium heat, in hot olive oil, cook green onions and carrots until tender, about 5 minutes, stirring frequently. Stir in dandelion greens, half-and-half cream, sea salt, cayenne and basil; heat to boiling. Remove saucepan from heat; stir in eggs.
Spoon mixture into loaf pan, cover with foil.
Place loaf pan into baking pan. Fill baking pan with hot water to come 1 in sides of loaf pan
Bake at 375°F for 1 ¼ hrs or until inserted knife comes out clean.
Spread on mashed potato, meat, bread, crackers or vegetables.

Remember when your mother said, "Eat your Greens".

Dandelion Pie

¼ cup olive oil
½ cup finely chopped onions
¼ cup finely chopped scallions
8 cups fresh dandelion, washed, drained and finely chopped
¼ cup finely cut fresh dill leaves
¼ cup finely chopped parsley
½ tsp. sea salt
Freshly ground black pepper
⅓ cup milk
½ lb. feta cheese, crumbled
4 eggs, lightly beaten
½ lb. butter melted or 8 oz. olive oil
16 sheets phyllo pastry

Heat olive oil in a heavy skillet. Add onions and scallions and cook, stirring frequently, until soft but not brown. Stir in dandelion, cover tightly and cook for 4 minutes. Add dill, parsley, sea salt and a few grindings of pepper while stirring and shaking pan. Cook uncovered for about 10 minutes – until most of the liquid has evaporated and dandelion sticks lightly to the pan.

Transfer to a bowl, add milk and cool to room temperature. Add cheese and slowly beat in the eggs. Taste for seasoning.

With a pastry brush, coat the bottom and sides of a 7" x 12" dish with olive oil. Line the dish with a sheet of phyllo, pressing the edges into the corners of the dish. Brush the surface of the pastry with 2 to 3 tsp. of olive oil. Continue until there are 8 layers of phyllo into the pan.

Spread the dandelion mixture on top of the phyllo. Place another layer of phyllo on top, coat with olive oil, and repeat, as before, until there are 8 layers. With scissors, trim the excess phyllo from around the edges of the dish. Brush top with remaining olive oil.
Bake pie at 300°F for about 1 hour, or until pastry is golden brown. Cut into squares and serve hot or at room temperature.

You might have your next goldmine in your yard.

Dandelion Squares

2-3 eggs
6 tbsp. whole wheat or spelt flour
3 ½ to 4 cups fresh dandelion
1 lb. cottage cheese
½ lb. grated Cheddar cheese
½ tsp. sea salt
3 tbsp. wheat germ or dark sesame seeds

Beat eggs and flour into a large bowl. Cut dandelion with scissors and add. Mix cottage cheese, Cheddar cheese and sea salt. Combine well. Pour into well-greased 9" x 13" baking pan and sprinkle with wheat germ or dark sesame seeds. Bake uncovered, at 350°F for approximately 45 minutes. Cut into squares for serving. Serves 6 to 8 Enjoy as an appetizer or with a meal.

Just imagine the build up of toxicity of sludge and decay, our human compost happening from out past diet. The eating of dandelion scares people, change is not easy, nor always comfortable. Awareness is the first step in addressing the problem.

Mini Dandelion Cups

3 ½ to 4 cups chopped dandelion, cooked, well drained
½ cup mozzarella cheese
⅓ cup cream cheese
1 tbsp. parmesan cheese
1 tbsp. finely chopped onion
¼ tsp. garlic powder
24 thin slices deli style turkey breast

Preheat oven to 350°F. Mix all ingredients except turkey until well blended.
Flatten turkey slices; place 1 slice in each of 24 miniature muffin pan cup. Fill each with 1 ½ tsp. of dandelion mixture
Bake 15 min or until heated through.
Serve warm.
Enjoy, I bet you can't eat just one.

May your life be like a wildflower; growing freely in the beauty and joy of each new day.
-Native American Proverb

Dandelion Stuffed Mushrooms

3 ½ to 4 cup scissor cut dandelion
24 medium to large mushrooms, cleaned and stemmed, reserving stems
Olive oil
½ cup grated parmesan cheese
⅔ cup crumbled feta cheese
½ cup finely chopped fresh parsley

Steam dandelion for 2 to 3 minutes, chop finely, and then drain well in sieve, pressing out moisture with wooden spoon. Finely chop mushroom stems and sauté in small amount of olive oil. Combine all ingredients, except mushroom caps, in bowl and mix well.

Brush outsides of mushroom caps with olive oil, and then fill with dandelion mixture, mounding it in the center. Place on baking sheet and bake at 375°F for 20 minutes or until mushrooms are soft. Serve warm. Makes 24

Feeling sluggish? Try all natural Dandelions to recharge your life and health.

Dandelion layered in Phyllo Sheets

3 tbsp. butter or olive oil
10 green onions or 1 large onion, chopped
4 cloves garlic, shopped
3 ½ to 4 cups dandelion, washed and chopped
2 tbsp. dried dill
2 tbsp. chopped fresh parsley
½ c grated feta cheese
4 large eggs
Sea salt and pepper
¾ cup olive oil
1 pkg. phyllo dough

Melt 3 tbsp. butter or olive oil in skillet; sauté onions and garlic until soft but not brown. Mix dandelion, dill and parsley. Cook over medium heat 5 minutes. Remove from heat and drain off any liquid in pan. Stir in cheese, eggs, sea salt and pepper. Brush a shallow pan with some of the olive oil. Remove 1 phyllo sheet from under tea towel. Lay it on a pan and brush with olive oil. Repeat, stacking the phyllo sheets until half of them have been used. Spread filling evenly over surface of stacked phyllo sheets.
Preheat oven to 375°F. You are now ready to make the top crust.
Stack phyllo sheets on top of filling, one by one, brushing each side with olive oil. Sprinkle with a few drops of water to prevent pastry from curling.
Bake about 45 minutes until top is golden brown. Cut into squares.

Makes 6 servings

"Where History meets Nature."

Party with Dandelion Rolls

½ cup chive and onion cream cheese
¼ cup feta crumbled cheese, sprinkled with oregano
4 flour tortillas
1 cup of cut up dandelion leaves
180g smoked salmon, thinly sliced

Mix cream cheese and feta cheese until well blended.
Spread evenly onto tortillas; top evenly with Salmon and dandelion.
Roll tortillas tightly; wrap individually in plastic wrap.
Refrigerate at least 2 hrs, or overnight.
Remove plastic wrap just before serving. Cut each roll crosswise into 12 pieces.
Arrange on serving plate.

Kids these days think the grocery store is the only place food comes from.

Dandelion Broccoli Bites

1 pkg. of stove top stuffing
½ cup of parmesan cheese
½ cup of milk
2 eggs
2 tbsp. of olive oil
1 pkg. of fresh frozen broccoli
1 cup of fine chopped dandelions
Dash of nutmeg

Mix and shape into balls and place on cookie sheet. Bake at 350°F for 15-20 min

ABC's of Dandelion

Aids - **B**abies
Children - Dandelion
Elderly - Fit People
Grown up's - History
Immunity - Joy
Kingdom - Love
Me - Naturally
O.K. - People
Queen Victoria - Raised Dandelions for
Supper - Toxins Eliminated
U feel better - Very Nice
Wellness - X-Generation
You get moving - Zambia needs some

Dandelion Balls

3 ½ to 4 cups dandelion, steamed and chopped
1 small onion, chopped
3 eggs
1 cup seasoned bread crumbs
¼ cup Parmesan cheese
Garlic salt to taste
Thyme to your taste
⅓ cup olive oil

Combine all ingredients and mix well. Form into small balls and freeze separately on a cookie sheet. Once it's frozen, place in an airtight container and use when required by baking at 350°F for approx 15 minutes. Serves 8 to 10 use as an appetizer.

Dandelions, they're the real deal!

Wilted Dandelion Greens

8 cups shredded dandelion greens
4 slices perchuto ham
1 tbsp. olive oil
2 tsp. sugar
½ tsp. sea salt
Dash of pepper
¼ tsp. dry mustard
3 tbsp. mild vinegar

Place greens in a large bowl.
Cook perchuto ham until crisp in olive oil. Remove from pan. Add remaining ingredients to the olive oil in the pan and heat, stirring until sugar is dissolved.
Pour mixture over dandelion greens and toss. Enjoy!

Taraxacum Officinale Latin for Dandelion means Cure for all Disorders.

Dandegreen & Egg Dishes

Dande Quiche

1 cup of grated Swiss cheese, cheddar cheese, or emmenthal cheese
1 piecrust
6 eggs
2 garlic cloves, crushed
1 cup of finely crumbled feta cheese
1 small finely minced onion or 3 green onions chopped
½ cup of finely chopped mushrooms
⅓ cup of chopped fresh basil
½ teaspoon of dry mustard powder
½ cup of milk (soy, goat, or rice milk can be substituted)
2 tablespoons of olive oil, your choice
¾ cup of sour cream or plain yogurt
3 ½ to 4 cups dandelion, chopped

Preheat oven to 400°F. Spread grated cheese over the bottom of the piecrust. In a bowl beat eggs, and add garlic, feta, onion, mushrooms, parsley, basil, dry mustard powder, milk, oil, and sour cream together. Mix in Dandelion. Pour dandelion, egg, mixture over the cheese in the bottom of the piecrust. Bake for 10 minutes at 400°F, then reduce heat to 325°F and bake until knife comes out of the center clean, approximately 30 minutes. Let cool for 10 minutes before slicing.
Enjoy sliced tomatoes on the side.

Dandelions get their nutrients from the ground, as do other vegetables we eat, like turnips, carrots, and potatoes etc.

Dandelion Quiche

4 oz. or approx ¼ cup of light cream cheese, softened
3 large eggs
2 cups chopped dandelion greens
1 cup grated medium cheddar cheese
10 oz. can, sliced mushrooms, drained
¼ cup chopped green onion
½ tsp. sea salt
⅛ tsp. ground nutmeg
½ cup low fat milk
Unbaked 9 inch pie crust
3 tbsp. grated parmesan cheese

Beat cream cheese and one egg together in bowl. Beat in remaining two eggs, one at a time.
Stir in next seven ingredients.
Pour into pie crust. Sprinkle with parmesan cheese. Bake on bottom oven rack at 350°F for 45 minutes until knife inserted in center comes out clean.
Serve with side salad. Feel the joy.

A sitcom on TV after supper, about the Dandy car, runs on Dandelions. It's implying or saying there's enough around to make use of them somehow, right!!!

Dandelion Feta Cheese Quiche

Pastry for 9-inch pie crust
2 tbsp. olive oil
½ cup finely chopped mushrooms
1 shallot, chopped
¼ cup pine nuts
2 cups finely chopped dandelion
2 eggs, beaten
¼ cup milk
Parmesan cheese
Nutmeg to taste

Heat olive oil sauté mushrooms, shallot and pine nuts. Steam the dandelion until limp, but still bright green. Beat together eggs, feta cheese, and milk. Add vegetables and spoon into pie crust. Top with Parmesan cheese and nutmeg. Bake at 350°F for 40 to 50 minutes. Enjoy as nature intended.

Make good use of the whole plant, as our universe has provided dandelions & eggs, food from the Gods.

Crab and Dandelion Quiche

1 pie crust
1 package (6 ounces) frozen crab meat
4 eggs
1 cup evaporated milk
1 tsp. prepared mustard
⅛ tsp. nutmeg
¾ tsp. sea salt
2 tbsp. dry sherry
2 cups chopped Dandelion leaves
¾ cup shredded Swiss cheese

Cook pasty. Set aside. Thaw crabmeat on microwave safe plate. Set aside. In large bowl, beat eggs. Add milk, mustard, nutmeg, sea salt, and sherry. Mix well. Drain dandelion. Pick over crabmeat and remove any cartilage. Add dandelion, cheese, and crabmeat to egg mixture. Stir well. Pour into pie crust. Cook on 350°F for 45 minutes until knife inserted into centre comes out clean.
Enjoy.

Surprise, Dandelions are edible, incredible.

The Lunch Omelet

½ to 1 tsp. coconut oil or olive oil for frying
2 eggs slightly beaten
2 green onions chopped
¼ cup of crumbled, feta or cheddar cheese.
1 handful of fresh picked cleaned and chopped dandelion leaves. (Or use frozen blanched dandelion in winter).

Cook over medium heat in a frying pan. Cut the omelet in 4 sections, flip once. Serve with a slice of rye toast.

Dandelion and eggs are good for you and it is one of my favorite meals.

Small lifestyle changes make a difference. Live the healthy life.

Dandelion Omelet for One

¼ cup fresh cut dandelion
1 egg
⅛ cup milk
2 tbsp. butter or extra virgin olive oil

Blend dandelion, egg and milk together. Melt butter or extra virgin olive oil in small frying pan over low heat. Pour omelet into frying pan. Lift edges toward the center as it cooks, to let the uncooked portion flow to the cooked portion. Cook until the bottom is light brown and the top is set. Fold half the omelet over the other half and serve.

If you are going to make this for the over two years old members of your family, spice it with nutmeg or chives or feta cheese.

Dandelions support our immune systems.

Dandelion and Sour Cream Omelet

3 cups dandelion greens
Sea salt
1½ tsp. olive oil
¼ tsp. nutmeg
Black pepper to taste
1 cup sour cream or low fat yogurt
Paprika & sumac
Eggs

Wash dandelion greens thoroughly. Drain. Place moist dandelion greens in a saucepan, sprinkle with sea salt and cover tightly. Cook over moderate heat, stirring once or twice. Drain and chop coarsely.
Add olive oil, nutmeg, additional sea salt and pepper to taste, and half the sour cream or low fat yogurt. Reheat gently over low heat without boiling.
Reserve six tbsp. of the mixture. Use the remaining as a filling for six three eggs omelets. Spoon the reserved mixture along the top of the folded omelet and top with remaining sour cream or low fat yogurt.
Sprinkle with paprika or sumac.

There's Abundance of Dandelions from Nature.

Dandelion and Bacon Omelet

1 tbsp. olive oil
⅓ cup thinly sliced green onion
½ cup sliced fresh white mushrooms
1 slice of bacon, cut into thin strips, or substitute sliced perchuto
1 cup dandelion greens
3 large eggs
1 tbsp. milk
Pinch of sea salt and pepper
1 tsp. olive oil
2 tbsp. grated cheddar cheese

Heat 1 tbsp. of olive oil in frying pan, on medium heat. Add green onion. Cook for 2-3 mins, stirring often, until softened. Add mushrooms and bacon. Cook for about 2 mins, stirring occasionally, until mushrooms are softened.
Add dandelion. Heat and stir for about 1 min until dandelion is wilted and liquid is almost evaporated.
Transfer to small bowl. Beat next 4 ingredients with whisk in separate bowl until smooth. Heat 1 tsp. of olive oil in same frying pan, on medium. Pour egg mixture into pan. Reduce heat to medium-low. When starting to set at outside edge, tilt pan and gently lift cooked egg with spatula, easing around pan from outside edge in. Allow uncooked egg to flow onto bottom of pan. Repeat, around pan, until egg is set.
Sprinkle cheese and dandelion mixture on ½ of omelet. Fold other ½ of omelet over dandelion mixture. Cover. Cook for about 2 mins or until cheese is melted.

Eat foods that heal, not harm!

Marble Dandelion Soufflé

Preheat oven to 350° F. Grease a 7 inch soufflé dish.
In saucepan, heat ⅓ cup olive oil.
Blend in a mixture of ⅓ cup flour, pinch of garlic salt and pepper.
Gradually stir in 1 ¼ c milk. Cook stirring constantly, until thickened.
Beat 6 egg yolks. Gradually blend in flour mixture.
In a large bowl, beat to form stiff but moist peaks, 6 egg whites, ½ tsp. sea salt, and ¼ tsp. cream of tartar.
Fold in egg yolk mixture.
Divide in half. In one half, fold 1 cup chopped fresh dandelion, 1 ½ tsp. chopped parsley.
Into the other half, fold a mixture of ½ cup marble cheese, grated, ¼ tsp. dry mustard.
Alternately spoon mixtures into prepared soufflé dish.
If desired, sprinkle with grated parmesan cheese.
Bake in 350°F oven for 55 min or until puffed and set.
Serve hot with cold roast beef, ham or turkey.

A chemist told me that the chemicals sprayed on dandelions to kill them one year, remains only 1 year. That's why they say you have to spray every year; therefore you should be able to eat the greens the next year. I have.

Lemon, Shrimp and Dandelion Crepes

2 tbsp. olive oil
1 garlic clove, minced
2 green onions, sliced
2 cups dandelion
1 ½ cups sliced mushrooms
1 tbsp. grated lemon rind
¼ cup flour
1 cup 1% milk
⅓ cup water
1 lb. cooked, peeled and divined shrimp
⅓ cup chopped fresh parsley
1 tbsp. lemon juice
Lemon pepper

Crepes:
2 egg whites
6 tbsp. flour
⅓ cup 1% milk

In small bowl, beat egg whites with flour. Gradually beat in milk. Spray 6-7 in omelet pan with cooking spray. Heat over medium-low heat. Pour about 3 tbsp. of batter into pan, swirling quickly to cover bottom. Cook until bottom is lightly browned. Flip crepe onto baking sheet. Repeat with remaining batter. Cover with tin foil to keep warm.
In saucepan, heat olive oil. Cook garlic, onion, dandelions, mushrooms and lemon rind. Cook until dandelion has wilted. Stir in flour. Gradually add milk and water. Cook stirring, until thickened. Stir in shrimp, parsley and lemon juice. Heat through.
Spoon 2 spoonful's of filling onto each shell. Fold over and sprinkle with lemon pepper.
Serve with sliced tomatoes or cut with vegetables. Enjoy.

"Harnessing the power of Nature"

Ham and Dandelion Soufflé

¼ cup finely diced ham
½ cup dandelion
1 tbsp. butter or olive oil
1 tsp. flour
¼ cup milk
1 egg separated

Cook dandelion. In saucepan melt butter or oil, add flour and stir.
Blend milk and egg yolk.
When mixture begins to thicken, stir in dandelion and ham.
Beat egg white until stiff and fold into mixture.
Pour into a buttered or oil soufflé dish and cook for 30 mins. at 350°F.

For those who like curry, serve ham and dandelion soufflé with hot curried fruit.

Pour 1- 6oz can of mixed fruit into a baking dish with 1 tsp. of curry. Sprinkle brown sugar or one of our healthier alternatives as seen in the back of this book over top and bake for 30 mins. at 350°F.

It's worth it,
You're worth it.

English Dandelion Eggs

3 ½ to 4 cups fresh dandelion
4 large eggs
1 tbsp. olive oil
2 tbsp. flour
½ pint of milk
2 tbsp. cream
⅓ cup grated cheddar cheese
2 tbsp. grated parmesan cheese
Sea salt, pepper, nutmeg

Rub olive oil over sides of a large shallow baking dish, arrange dandelion over the base, season with pepper, sea salt and nutmeg. Then sprinkle 1 tbsp. of cream over and put into lower part of oven to heat through.
Now place the olive oil, milk, and flour in saucepan and whisk over heat to make a smooth white sauce. Then stir in grated cheddar cheese and cook sauce for 3 mins. over gentle heat, stirring occasionally.
Now, take the baking dish out of oven, make four depressions in dandelion and gently break eggs into each one. Stir the remaining tbsp. of cream into cheese sauce and pour over eggs to cover. Sprinkle with parmesan cheese and bake for 15-20 min on 375°F.

Dandelions, that's for life.

Danish Dandelion Ring

8 cups of scissor cut dandelion greens
¼ cup cream or milk
4 eggs, beaten
½ tsp. sea salt
½ tsp. sugar

Wash dandelion greens well and place in a deep saucepan. Cover and cook, without additional water, until tender, about 2 mins.
Add cream and heat to simmering. Do not boil. Stir a little of dandelion into the eggs, then return mixture to pot. Add sea salt.
Turn into a greased ring mold. Place on a rack in a pot and surround with a little boiling water. Cover pot and steam about 30 mins. Or set in a pan of boiling water and bake in a 350°F oven until set.
The ring is done when a knife inserted in center comes out clean.

Dandelions are wild, handpicked, additive free, 100% natural, grown in native soil, Natural Vitamins and Mineral sources.

Dandelion Bake

3 eggs
1 ½ cups cottage cheese
1 cup grated cheddar cheese, mixed with grated Swiss cheese
¼ cup olive oil
½ tsp. sea salt, pepper
Pinch of nutmeg
1 ¼ cups dandelion greens, cooked and drained

Beat eggs in bowl. Mix in cottage, Swiss and cheddar cheeses, olive oil, sea salt, pepper and nutmeg.
Add drained dandelion to egg mixture. Stir.
Pour into a 2 qt. casserole. Cover and bake at 350°F for 45 to 55 mins.
Casserole is done when knife inserted comes out clean.
Nice for lunch served with salad.

Beat depression with dandelions.

Dandelion Tarts

½ cup olive oil or softened butter
4 oz. or ¼ cup of cream cheese, softened
1 cup flour

Beat olive oil or butter and cream cheese together until smooth. Work in flour. Shape into long roll. Mark off, and then cut into 24 pieces. Press into small tart tins to form shells

Filling
1 egg
½ cup grated cheddar cheese
½ cup cooked, chopped dandelion greens, drained
¼ cup sour cream or low fat yogurt
¼ cup milk
¼ tsp. onion salt
¼ tsp. sea salt

Beat egg until frothy. Stir in remaining ingredients spoon into shells.
Bake at 350°F for 20-25 min until set.
Share and enjoy.

When your body is overburdened by toxins, it can result in decreased metabolism, bloating, digestive disorders and a dramatic decrease in your energy levels.

Dandelion Pie

2 ½ cups chopped dandelion greens
Sea salted water
1 cup chopped onion
2 tbsp. olive oil
6 eggs
1 cup feta cheese, crumbled
1 tsp. parsley flakes
½ tsp. prepared mustard
¼ tsp. garlic powder
¼ tsp. oregano
⅛ tsp. pepper
1 lb. phyllo pastry
¼ cup olive oil

Cook dandelion greens in sea salted water for a couple of minutes. Drain well.
Sauté onions in olive oil until soft and clear.
Beat eggs. Add cheese, parsley, mustard, garlic powder, sea salt, pepper and oregano. Mix. Add dandelion greens and onion. Stir together.
Brush 10 inch pie plate with olive oil. Layer with 8 sheets phyllo pastry and brush each sheet with olive oil. As you do so spoon dandelion mixture on top. Cover with 8 more sheets of pastry, brushing each with olive oil. Score top sheets into wedges but do not cut right through all top sheets. Trim edge. Bake at 375°F for 50 mins.
Cuts into 8 wedges
Enjoy for supper with a side of your favorite vegetable.

Dandelions create natural healing for your next digestive drama.

Italian Dandelion Pie

10 oz. cottage cheese
2 ½ cups chopped dandelion greens, washed, well drained
1 cup shredded mozzarella cheese
4 eggs, beaten
3 tbsp. chopped roasted red peppers
⅓ cup grated parmesan cheese
1 tsp. oregano

Quickly stir all ingredients together.
Pour into 9 inch pie plate.
Bake at 350°F for 40 min or until center is set.
Enjoy anytime.

Dandelions stimulate bile production which in turn resolves constipation.

Dandegreens in Pasta

Mediterranean Chicken and Dandelion Pasta Bake

8 boneless, skinless chicken thighs, trimmed and halved
1 tbsp. olive oil
4 cups cut dandelion leaves
1 pkg. minestrone or vegetable soup mix (you may want add ¼ to ½ cup of your choice of pasta, especially if you use the vegetable soup mix)
1 can diced tomatoes (28 oz.)
1 tbsp. dried or ¼ cup chopped fresh basil
2 tbsp. finely sliced, pitted black olives
1 cup shredded mozzarella cheese

Preheat oven to 350°F. In a large, non-stick skillet set over medium-high heat; brown the chicken in olive oil. Remove the chicken from the skillet and arrange in a single layer in a well-greased 8-inch (20 cm) baking dish. Place the dandelion evenly over the chicken. Next, you combine minestrone or vegetable soup mix and (pasta, optional) with the tomatoes, basil, and black olives. Spread the mixture evenly over top of the dandelion. Try to keep the pasta submerged in the liquid, if you have added it. Cover with foil and bake for 55 minutes. Uncover and sprinkle with cheese. Bake 10-15 minutes more or until the cheese is bubbly.

Healthy eating, it's for life.

Picnic Time Macaroni Salad

¼ cup minced onion
¼ cup celery
½ cup ranch salad dressing
½ cup low fat yogurt
1 tbsp. lemon juice
¼ cup sour cream
1 tsp. black pepper
1 tsp. parsley
1 tsp. cayenne pepper or to your taste
1 tsp. garlic powder
4 cups pasta of choice, cooked in water, drained and cooled
½ cup chopped dandelion greens per person
1 cup yellow pepper, diced

Mix first 10 ingredients well until smooth and evenly coated. Add pasta
Place ½ cup of dandelion greens as a bed for the salad, on each plate.
On each bed of dandelion place a portion of salad.
For added flare with color, top off each person's plate with 1 tbsp. diced yellow pepper.

Treat the earth well.
It was not given to you by your parents,
It was loaned to you by your children.
We do not inherit the Earth from our Ancestors,
We borrow it from our children.
Ancient Indian Proverb.

Dandegreen Pasta Primavera

500 grams spaghetti or fettuccini
3 cups prewashed dandelion
1 red pepper
1 yellow pepper
1 can whole mushrooms
1 tub of light garden vegetable spreadable cream cheese
½ cup milk
2 tbsp. fresh minced basil
Parmesan cheese to taste

Cook 500 g of spaghetti or fettuccine in boiling water, adding 10 oz. of pre-washed fresh dandelion, 1 each thinly sliced red and yellow peppers, and 1 can whole mushrooms to the water for the last 3 to 6 minutes of the cooking time, drain.
Spoon 1 tub (250g) of light garden vegetable cream cheese into the hot pan and add about ½ cup milk.
Cook and stir over low heat until smooth.
Add the pasta and 2 tbsp. fresh minced basil and toss with sauce.
Sprinkle with parmesan grated cheese.

Serves 8

Make the natural choice, eat dandelions.

Greek Pasta with Dandelion and Tomatoes

2 cups of rotini pasta
½ cup of vegetable stock
1 clove of garlic chopped
1 small onion chopped
2 medium tomatoes
2 cups of chopped dandelions leaves
½ cup of black olives
½ cup of tomatoes
½ tsp. of dried oregano or 2 tbsp. of chopped fresh oregano
½ tsp. of black pepper
½ tsp. of sea salt

Makes 4-6 servings, preparation time 10 min. Cooking time 15 min

In the pot, cook the rotini in boiling water for about 7 to 8 min. Drain pasta and set aside.
In the sauté pan, heat the garlic and onion for about 3-4 min, then add the vegetable stock. Add all the other ingredients and simmer the sauce on low heat for about 5 min.
Add the pasta to the sauce mix and blend well before serving.

Hint you can replace olives with ½ cup of sun dried tomatoes.

Eating green is a logical necessity.

Dande Lasagna

16 cooked lasagna noodles
2 tbsp. olive oil
1 small onion, chopped
3 ½ to 4 cups dandelions
1 (7 oz.) container pesto
2 (15 oz.) containers ricotta cheese
1 egg
½ tsp. sea salt
¼ tsp. nutmeg
¼ tsp. pepper
2 cups shredded mozzarella cheese
1 (9 oz.) container Alfredo sauce
¼ cup parmesan cheese

Heat oven to 350°F spray 3 quart glass baking dish with nonstick cooking spray. Heat olive oil in large skillet over medium heat until hot.
Add onion; cook 3 to 5 minutes or until tender, stirring occasionally.
Add dandelion; stir to combine. Remove from heat.
Stir in pesto.
In large bowl, combine ricotta cheese, eggs, sea salt, nutmeg and pepper; mix well.
Layer 4 cooked noodles in baking dish. Cover the noodles with 1/2 the dandelions. Spread ⅓ of ricotta mixture over dandelion. Sprinkle with ⅓ of mozzarella cheese. Repeat layers ending with noodles. Spread Alfredo sauce over top of noodles. Sprinkle with parmesan cheese. Cover baking dish with foil.
Bake lasagna for 45 to 55 minutes or until thoroughly heated.

8 servings

Dandelion is an herb with medicinal properties

Dandelion Vegetables and Pasta Parmesan or Cheddar

2 stalks of celery chopped
1 small onion
1 small bell pepper chopped
3 cups vegetable stock
2 cups of fusilli {spiral pasta} uncooked
1 cup of canned diced tomatoes
½ cup of grated carrot
½ tsp. of black pepper
½ tsp. of dried basil or 1 tbsp. chopped fresh basil
½ tsp. dried thyme or 1 tbsp. of chopped fresh thyme
½ tsp. of sea salt
½ cup of parmesan cheese or shredded cheddar cheese
Add 1 cup of cut up dandelions to the last 3 min. of boiling.

Easy one pot pasta, 10 min preparation, 15 min. cook time. You can add or delete ingredients as you like. Enjoy.

In the pot combine all the ingredients, except dandelions and parmesan cheese. Bring the mixture to a boil on high heat. Immediately reduce the heat to medium and simmer for about 15 min or until pasta is cooked.
Mix in dandelions and sprinkle with parmesan cheese and serve.

Healthy thoughts come from inside.

Dandelion and Squash Lasagna

1 large butternut squash (about 4 lb.)
2 tbsp. extra-virgin olive oil
½ tsp. sea salt
¼ tsp. pepper
16 lasagna noodles
1 cup of fresh dandelions
3 cups shredded mozzarella cheese

Dande Tomato Sauce

4 oz. pancetta or lean bacon, chopped
1 onion, finely chopped
1 stalk celery, finely chopped
2 cloves garlic, minced
¼ tsp. hot pepper flakes, optional
1 can or 280 oz. diced tomatoes
½ cup dry red wine
¼ cup tomato paste
1 ½ tsp. each dried oregano and sage

Dande Cheese Sauce

¼ cup butter, olive oil or coconut oil
½ cup all-purpose flour
3 cups milk
1 ½ cups grated parmesan cheese
½ tsp. nutmeg
2 eggs, lightly beaten

Peel squash, cut into ¼ inch thick slices. Brush bottom sides with oil. Place on 2 foil-lined rimmed baking sheets. Sprinkle with ½ tsp. of the sea salt and pepper. Roast in 350°F oven until tender and lightly browned, about 30 minutes. Let cool in pans.

(Continued on next page)

Dande Tomato Sauce
Meanwhile, on large nonstick skillet, fry pancetta over medium heat until fat begins to release; drain off fat. Stir in onion, celery, garlic and hot pepper flakes, optional; cook until vegetables soften, about 3 minutes. Add diced tomatoes, red wine, tomato paste, oregano and sage; reduce heat to low and simmer, stirring occasionally, until thickened, about 30 minutes. Set aside.

Dande Cheese Sauce

In saucepan, melt butter, olive oil or coconut oil over medium heat; stir in flour and cook, stirring, for 4 minutes. Gradually whisk in milk; cook, whisking constantly until bubbly. Boil for 5 minutes, whisking often. Remove from heat. Whisk in parmesan cheese and nutmeg; blend in eggs. Set aside.

In large pot of boiling sea salted water, cook noodles until almost tender, 6-8 minutes. Drain and chill in cold water; arrange in a single layer on damp tea towel.
Rinse dandelion' shake off excess water. In large saucepan, cook dandelion, with just the water clinging to the leaves, over medium-high heat until wilted, about 5 minutes; drain in colander. Squeeze out liquid; chop dandelion and season with remaining sea salt.

Spread half of the tomato sauce in baking dish. Top with single layer of noodles, cutting to fit. Top with half of the squash. Spread with half of the cheese sauce; sprinkle with half of the mozzarella. Repeat noodle layer, remaining tomato sauce, then layer with dandelion greens, and then remaining squash. Top with remaining cheese sauce. Sprinkle with the remaining mozzarella.
Cover loosely with foil. Bake on rimmed baking sheet in 375°F oven for 25 minutes. Uncover and bake until bubbly and cheese is lightly browned, about 20 or so minutes. Let stand 10 minutes.

You got to love what dandelions do for you, you just got to get them to the table. They do the rest.

Quick Dandelion, Tomato & Rice

1 large can of tomato juice
½ tsp. onion powder
½ tsp. celery powder
½ tsp. garlic powder
2 cups cooked rice
Large bunch, 2 to 4 cups of dandelions cut up in bite size pieces.

Put everything but dandelions into large pot and heat through.
Add dandelions 3-5 minutes, before serving.

We need to help fund & promote Wellness in a Natural way, with Good Nutrition.

Dandelion-Beef Spaghetti Pie

6 oz. uncooked angel hair pasta
2 eggs, lightly beaten
⅓ cup grated Parmesan cheese
1 lb. ground beef
½ cup chopped onion
¼ cup chopped green pepper
14 oz. spaghetti sauce
1 tsp. Creole seasoning (optional)
¾ tsp. garlic powder
½ tsp. dried basil
½ tsp. dried oregano
8 oz. cream cheese, softened
3 cups chopped dandelion greens
½ cup shredded mozzarella cheese

Cook pasta according to pkg., drain. Add eggs and parmesan cheese. Press into bottom and sides of deep dish pie plate. Bake at 350°F for 10 mins.
Meanwhile, in skillet, cook beef, onion and green pepper, drain. Stir in spaghetti sauce and seasonings. Bring to a boil. Reduce heat; cover and simmer for 10 mins.
Between 2 pieces of waxed paper, roll out cream cheese into a 7 inch circle. Place in pasta crust. Top with dandelion and meat sauce. Sprinkle with mozzarella cheese
Bake at 350°F for 20-30 minutes or until set.

Dandelions... the power of nature

Tomato and Dandelion Pasta

1 lb or 3 to 4 cups spiral pasta
2 tbsp. olive oil
3 cloves garlic, chopped
3 ½ to 4 cups fresh dandelion greens, cleaned and chopped
1 cup fresh basil, coarsely chopped
¼ cup sun-dried tomatoes, chopped
18 tomatoes, cored, seeded and cut in halves
¼ cup freshly grated parmesan cheese
1 to 2 cups of leftover meat (optional bacon)

Prepare pasta according to package, drain water.
Heat your olive oil in large skillet, over medium heat.
Add garlic and sauté until golden, about one minute.
Add dandelion greens in handfuls. Watch it wilt.
Add basil, sun-dried tomatoes and any other leftover cooked meat (optional).
Stir to combine for one minute, or until heated through.
Add the hot cooked pasta and the heated dandelion mixture in large bowl.
Stir in tomatoes and cheese.
Serve immediately.

Eat dandelions, control your blood sugar.

Dandelion Pasta Salad

2 tbsp. lemon juice
1 tbsp. olive oil
1 garlic clove, minced
½ lb. boneless, skinless chicken halves
2 cups medium bow pasta
4 cups dandelion greens, lightly packed
1 cup chopped tomato
½ cup coarsely crumbled feta cheese
⅓ cup olives without the pit

Parsley Pesto Dressing
½ cup coarsely chopped parsley
⅓ cup Parmesan cheese
⅓ cup olive oil
¼ cup pine nuts, toasted
¼ cup red wine vinegar
2 cloves garlic, minced
¼ tsp. sea salt and pepper

Combine lemon juice, olive oil and garlic in medium bowl. Add chicken. Turn until coated. Preheat electric grill for 5 mins. Cook chicken on greased grill for 5 mins. per side until no longer pink inside. Let stand 10 mins. Cut into thick slices. Keep warm.
Cook pasta according to pkg. Drain. Rinse under cold water. Drain well. Transfer to large bowl.
Add chicken and the rest of ingredients, including the parsley pesto dressing. Toss gently, serve and enjoy.

Dandelions for starvation

Dandelion Cheese Cannelloni

1 onion, finely chopped
3 garlic cloves, minced
1 tbsp. olive oil
2 cups ricotta cheese
1 cup shredded mozzarella cheese
6 tbsp. grated parmesan cheese
1 tsp. oregano seasoning
½ tsp. ground pepper
3 cups chopped dandelion greens
8 cannelloni shells, cooked and drained
26 oz. jar of spaghetti sauce

In small skillet, sauté onion and garlic in oil for 3 minutes, set aside. In mixing bowl, combine ricotta, ½ cup mozzarella, 4 tbsp. Parmesan cheese, oregano seasoning and pepper; beat until smooth. Stir the dandelion into the 3 cheeses, and add to the seasoned cooked onion mixture. Spoon this into the cooked cannelloni shells.
Pour half of spaghetti sauce into a greased baking dish. Arrange stuffed pasta shells over sauce; top with remaining sauce. Cover and bake at 350°F for 25 mins. Uncover; sprinkle with remaining mozzarella and Parmesan cheese.
Bake 5-10 minutes longer or until cheese has melted.

"Food" can make your "Mood"

Homemade Dandelion Noodles

3 cups fresh dandelion greens
Water
Sea salt
2 eggs
2 ½ – 3 cups flour
1 tbsp. salad oil
Butter or olive oil to toss

Wash dandelion greens; trim of tough ribs and stems. In saucepan over medium heat, heat to boiling ¼ inch water and ½ tsp. sea salt. Add dandelion and return to boiling; cover and cook 3 mins. Drain well; blot excess moisture with paper towels. Puree dandelion with blender and place in large bowl.
With fork, stir eggs, 2 ½ cups flour and 1 tsp. sea salt until mixture resembles coarse crumbs. Shape dough into ball. On well-floured surface, knead until smooth and not sticky, about 10 mins. Wrap in waxed paper; let stand 30 mins; cut dough into 2 equal pieces.
On floured surface with rolling pin, roll half of dough into rectangle. Use a knife, cut into strips. Place in single layer on clean cloth towels. Repeat with remaining dough. Let noodles strips dry at least 2 hrs.

About 20 minutes before serving:
In saucepan, over high heat, heat to boiling, 4 quarts water, 2 tbsp. sea salt and 1 tbsp. olive oil. Add noodles and return to boiling; cook 8 minutes or until tender but firm. In colander, drain noodles; return to pot. Add butter or olive oil; toss until melted.
Serve on heated platter with sliced tomato on side of plate.

Dandelions are good nutrition

Dandelion and Sweet Potato Pasta

1 tbsp. olive oil
1 cup chopped onion
1 ½ cups sliced fresh white mushrooms
2 garlic cloves, minced
1 tbsp. olive oil
2 tbsp. flour
1 cup prepared vegetable broth
½ cup white wine
3 cups chopped sweet potato
1 tsp. rosemary
¼ tsp. sea salt and pepper
2 cups fresh scissor cut dandelion greens
½ cup prepared vegetable broth
⅓ cup chopped green onion
¼ cup sour cream or low fat yogurt
1 tbsp. Dijon mustard with whole seeds
2 cups penne pasta
Grated parmesan cheese

Add first amount of olive oil in frying pan on medium heat. Add onion. Cook 5-10 minutes, stirring often, until softened.
Add mushrooms and garlic. Cook 3-5 minutes stirring occasionally until mushrooms are softened. Transfer to slow cooker.
Melt second amount of olive oil in same frying pan on medium. Add flour. Heat and stir for 1 minute. Slowly add first amount of broth, stirring constantly until smooth. Add wine. Heat and stir for about 3 minutes until boiling and thickened. Add the thickened broth to the mushroom mixture already in the slow cooker. Stir.

Add next 4 ingredients. Stir well. Cover and cook on low for 6-7 hrs. or on high for 3 - 3 ½ hrs. Mash yams slightly.
Add next 5 ingredients. Stir well. Cover and cook on high for 10 mins. until dandelion is wilted.
Cook pasta according to pkg. Drain. Return pasta to pot. Add sweet potato mixture. Toss until coated. Add parmesan cheese. Stir gently.

Dandelions - a natural detox.

Pasta with Lemon and Dandelion

4 cups penne pasta
1 tbsp. olive oil
1 clove garlic, minced
1 cup light ricotta cheese
¼ cup grated Parmesan cheese
1 tsp. grated lemon rind
2 tbsp. lemon juice
½ tsp. sea salt and pepper
3 cups fresh dandelion greens
½ cup finely diced sweet red pepper

Cook pasta according to pkg. Reserve ½ cup of cooking liquid, drain pasta and set aside.
In same saucepan, add olive oil over medium heat; fry garlic until fragrant. Add reserved cooking liquid, ricotta cheese, half of the Parmesan cheese, lemon rind and juice, sea salt and pepper; bring to a simmer.
Add dandelion greens cut in bite size pieces and the diced red pepper, stir until dandelion is wilted. Return pasta to pot and toss to coat.
Sprinkle with remaining Parmesan cheese.
Enjoy.

"Break through disease", with Dandelions

Dandegreen Salads

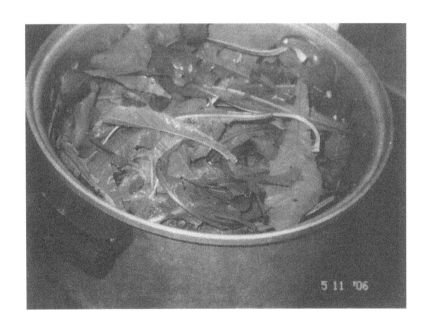

Wilted Green Salad

6 cups torn leaf lettuce
6 cups scissor cut fresh dandelion greens
2 green onions, sliced
¼ cup cider vinegar
2 tbsp. water
2 tbsp. olive oil
2 tsp. sugar
4 turkey-bacon strips, cooked and crumbled

In large salad bowl, toss lettuce, dandelion and onions; set aside. In small saucepan, bring vinegar, water, olive oil and sugar to a boil. Pour over salad and toss; sprinkle with crumbled turkey-bacon.

Natural Dying for purple = dandelion, tin & vinegar
Magenta = dandelion & Alum

Wilted Dandelion Side Salad

2 cups cut dandelion greens, lightly packed
4 tsp. white vinegar
2 tsp. water
1 green onion, sliced
1 bacon slice, cooked crisp and then crumbled, or use leftover chicken or turkey
1 tsp. sugar
Pinch of pepper
1 hard-boiled egg, grated or finely chopped

Place dandelion greens in bowl.
Measure next 7 ingredients into small saucepan.
Heat and stir until boiling.
Pour over dandelion greens.
Stir well to wilt.
Can be doubled to share

Friendship D-Tea
Upon ingesting – you will find Joy in the roots of Dandelions

Dandelion Squash Salad

1 ½ cups sliced peeled butternut squash, cut into ⅛ inch thick slices
12 medium white mushrooms, halved
3 cups of dandelion greens, stems removed
6 thin deli ham slices, cooked crisp and broken into ¾ inch pieces
½ cup shaved fresh Parmesan cheese

Apple Spice Dressing
¼ cup olive oil
2 tbsp. apple cider vinegar
1 clove garlic, minced
⅛ tsp. ground nutmeg and cinnamon
 Sea salt and pepper

Spray both sides of each side of squash with cooking spray (or grease both sides with olive oil).
Preheat electric grill for 5 minutes. Cook squash on well-greased grill for 5 mins per side until tender and browned.
Cut into ¾ inch pieces. Put into large bowl.
Spray mushrooms with cooking spray. Cook on greased grill for about 5 minutes, turning once, until browned. Cut in half and add to squash.
Add dandelion greens and ham. Toss with the apple dressing Scatter cheese over top. Enjoy.

Imagine no Obesity...

Apple Dandelion Salad

2 cups dandelion greens
1 apple, thinly sliced
2 tbsp. chopped celery
2 tbsp. toasted pecans, chopped or substitute sunflower seeds
2 tbsp. honey Dijon dressing

Toss ingredients with dressing in large bowl and serve

As Grandma Warner used to say, "An Apple a day, keeps the doctor Away"

Dandelions why Care? Healthcare

Dandelion Apple-Chicken Salad

2 cups cubed, cooked chicken breast
2 cups apples, cored and cubed
2 tbsp. lime juice
2 tbsp. apple, orange or carrot juice
1 ½ tbsp. non-fermented soy sauce
1 tbsp. mirin or rice wine
1 piece fresh ginger, finely grated
¼ cup chopped fresh parsley
3 scallions, thinly sliced
3 ½ to 4 cups dandelion
⅛ cup olive oil

Put the chicken and apples in a large bowl. In small bowl, mix together the lime juice, apple juice, olive oil, soy sauce, mirin or rice wine and ginger, and pour over the top of the apples and chicken, gently toss to mix (cover and refrigerate up to several hours, if desired).
To serve, layer the dandelion on a plate and spoon the chicken mixture on top.
Makes four servings

Some think it tastes bad but it works

Dande Sprout Salad

½ cup shredded dandelion
2 chopped scallions
2 cups mixed sprouts (bean, alfalfa, radish, pea, or lentil)
½ tsp oregano or marjoram
1 tbsp. vinaigrette dressing

In a large bowl mix the Dandelion, scallions, sprouts and oregano or marjoram. Add 1 tbsp. of your favorite bottle vinaigrette dressing – or make your own by combining 3 parts olive oil 1 part vinegar, 1 tsp. Dijon mustard in a jar and shake it. Toss well with the greens and serve.

Dandelions: the first food for Bees in spring.

Dandelion Salad

3 ½ to 4 cups dandelion greens
Sea salt
2 tbsp. lemon juice
6 tbsp. olive oil
Black pepper
2 hard cooked eggs cut into wedges
1 large tomato, cut into wedges
½ red onion, sliced

Wash dandelion greens and chill in a damp, clean cloth. Scissor cut into bite sized pieces.
Sprinkle bottom of salad bowl with lemon juice and olive oil and chill bowl.
When ready to serve, add dandelion greens and sprinkle with sea salt and pepper. Garnish with egg and tomato wedges and red onion.
Toss lightly and serve.

Dandelions are good to re-alkaline you, opposite of being too acidic inside.

Dandelion Slaw

2 cups of fresh dandelions
⅓ lb. cabbage washed and trimmed
¼ cup seedless raisins, optional.
5 tbsp. lemon juice
3 ¾ tbsp olive oil
Sea salt, pepper, sugar to taste
1 apple cored and chopped

Remove any coarse stems from dandelions. Wash in cold water. Pat leaves dry on tea towel. Finely shred dandelion and cabbage. Soak raisins in half of lemon juice until soft and swollen, and then add to dandelions and cabbage.
Beat together oil, remaining lemon juice, sea salt, pepper and sugar to taste. Add apple and pour over salad. Toss lightly to coat.
Enjoy beside your favorite meat or fish.

We clean our bodies on the outside, why not do some cleaning on the inside

Wilted Green Salad

10 cups leaf lettuce
6 cups cut fresh dandelion greens
2 green onions, sliced
¼ cup cider vinegar
2 tbsp. water
2 tbsp. olive oil
2 tsp. sugar
4 turkey bacon strips, cooked and crumbled, or any leftover meat

In large salad bowl, toss lettuce, dandelion and onions, set aside. In small saucepan, bring vinegar, water, oil, and sugar to a boil. Pour over lettuce and toss. Sprinkle with bacon, turkey, or leftover meat. Enjoy.

Popeye ate spinach greens! Debbie eats dandelion greens!

Dande Reuben Salad

8 cups scissor cut dandelions
1 large tomato, cut into wedges
1 cup croutons
½ lb. deli corned beef, sliced, cut into strips
¾ cup cubed Swiss cheese
¼ cup drained sauerkraut
¼ cup Thousand Island dressing

Combine greens, tomato and croutons in a large serving bowl. Add remaining ingredients; toss lightly.

Serves four

"Oh Adam was a gardener and God who made him sees that half a proper gardeners work is done on his knees"
-Rudyard Kipling

Tasty Salad Dressings for your Dandelion Salad

⅓ cup of olive oil
¼ cup vinegar
¼ tsp. Tabasco sauce
¼ tsp. dry mustard
½ tsp. sea salt
1 clove of garlic, crushed

Mix ingredients well. Enjoy over your cleaned, cut dandelions. Store the leftovers in fridge.

Jan's Salad Dressing for Dandelions

½ cup of brown sugar, packed
½ cup cream or milk
¼ cup vinegar

Add pepper to taste.

Many of the plants that we now consider garden weeds were eaten by the first European settlers in America. In fact, many of these dandelions were introduced here as a valuable source of food.

Dandelion Shallot Salad

This is best made with young dandelions. The hot dressing cooks the salad slightly and helps to soften the leaves.

2 cups young dandelions
3 oz. pancetta (Italian bacon)
1 tbsp. olive oil
1 tbsp. finely diced shallots
2 tbsp. sherry vinegar or sherry or red wine vinegar
2 tbsp. white wine
Freshly ground pepper

Wash and dry well, then cut up the dandelions.
Place in a large bowl, cut the pancetta into small slices. Heat the olive oil in a frying pan, add the pancetta.
Cook gently until it renders all of its fat and becomes crispy.

Remove the pancetta and drain on paper towel. Add the shallots to the fat and cook until transparent. Add the vinegar, stirring to incorporate any of the browned pieces from the bottom of the frying pan. Add the white wine and season with pepper (the pancetta provides enough salt).

Pour the hot dressing over the dandelion leaves, toss and serve immediately.

Serves 4 to 6

To my knowledge Dandelions are still free. You can be free, also.

Spring Dandelion Salad

2 cups of cut up dandelion leaves
3 wild leeks, chopped
¼ cup sunflower seeds
2 - 3 fresh basil leaves
¼ cup olive oil
¼ cup of cider vinegar
1 tbsp. of lemon juice
2 tsp. of sugar, more or less to taste
½ tsp. of Worcestershire sauce

Combine cleaned watercress, dandelion leaves add leeks, sunflower seeds and basil, toss together.
Combine remaining ingredients, pour over salad and toss well.
Enjoy!

The dandelion greens are high in vitamin A & C, and have high levels of iron, calcium, phosphorus, potassium, magnesium and copper.

Dandelion and Mushroom Salad

3 ½ cups of scissor cut dandelion leaves
⅓ cup of mushroom slices
4 thick rings of red bell pepper
¼ cup drained canned garbanzo beans

Divide the dandelions between 2 individual salad bowls or plates. Arrange the mushrooms, pepper rings, and garbanzo beans over the dandelions.

Serve with sweet and spicy French dressing.

Sweet and Spicy French dressing (yields ¾ cup)

2 tbsp. chopped onions
½ cup apple juice
3 tbsp. white wine vinegar
2 tbsp. tomato paste
1 clove garlic
½ tsp. paprika
¼ tsp. chili powder
¼ tsp. sea salt
Dash cayenne pepper to taste

Place all the ingredients in a blender and process for 1 min.
Transfer the dressing to a small bowl, cover and chill before serving.

Dandelion greens make an excellent substitute for spinach

Spinach/Dandelion Salad

1 cup of leftover chicken or turkey
3 ½ to 4 cups spinach and dandelion torn or cut
3 hardboiled eggs chopped
¾ cup garlic dressing

Cut or tear dandelion and spinach into salad bowl. Sprinkle meat and eggs on top. Pour dressing over and toss gently. Serve immediately

Garlic dressing

1 cup olive oil
Soak ½ clove of garlic in oil for 1 hour before mixing
¼ cup vinegar
¼ cup lemon juice
1 tsp. sea salt
½ tsp. dry mustard
½ tsp. paprika
Shake together.

You are going to notice the benefits of eating dandelions.

Dandelion Salad

4 cups dandelion leaves
½ small red or white onion cut in crescents or half moons
1 tomato cut in eighths
Olive oil and vinegar dressing

Wash dandelion greens and scissor cut into bite size pieces. Toss with onion and tomato.
Drizzle with olive oil and vinegar dressing and serve immediately.

Olive oil and Vinegar Dressing
½ cup olive oil
3 tbsp. wine vinegar or lemon juice
1 tbsp. Dijon mustard
3 cloves garlic, minced
Sea salt and pepper to taste

Shake ingredients together in a small jar.

This knowledge about Dandelions is a gift of good health.
"One man's weed is another man's livelihood." Raymond Loo, Big P.E.I. potato and dandelion farmer. He sells dandelions to the Japanese

Dandelion Cheese Salad

4 cups fresh dandelion
½ lb. mushrooms
½ lb. cottage cheese or grated cheese
1 red onion
⅔ cup olive oil
⅓ cup red wine vinegar
Oregano, sea salt and ground black pepper to taste

Wash dandelion and pat leaves dry with a tea towel. Scissor cut into pieces.
Clean, trim and thickly slice mushrooms. Add your favorite cheese and peel, quarter and thinly slice red onion.
Combine dandelion, mushrooms, cheese and onions in a large mixing bowl. Whisk together the olive oil, vinegar, oregano and a little sea salt. Pour the dressing over the salad and toss gently until every leaf is evenly coated. Grind some black pepper over the salad and toss again lightly.
.

The sun shines on it and the rain nurtures it.

Dandelions, Watercress & Mushroom Warm Salad

2 bunches or 8 cups dandelion washed & scissor cut
1 bunch or 4 cups watercress washed & scissor cut
½ lb. of mushrooms, sliced
½ lb. of lean bacon, diced or leftover cooked turkey or chicken
2 eggs
1 tbsp. sugar
6 tbsp. vinegar
2 tbsp. chopped dill

Toss dandelion and watercress with mushrooms. Fry bacon until crisp. Or better yet, use leftover meat. Whip eggs lightly and stir in sugar, vinegar and dill. Pour off all but 2 tbsp. bacon drippings, or use 2 tbsp. of olive oil in skillet. Pour egg mixture into skillet. Cook stirring, until it thickens. Pour over greens and serve warm. 4-6 servings

The difficulties with redefining history; dandelions have been in the making for years. In Victorian era, people grew dandelions along with their lettuces in their gardens.

Dandegreen Salad with Creamy Curry Mustard Dressing

8 cups of fresh dandelion leaves, washed, dried & scissor cut
1 to 2 tart apples, peeled cored and roughly chopped
3 scallions, finely minced (white and green parts included)

Curry mustard dressing:
¾ cup of plain low-fat yogurt
1 ½ tbsp. of olive oil
2 tsp. of lemon juice
½ tsp. of curry powder or to taste
1 tsp. of Dijon mustard
Sea salt and freshly ground white pepper to taste

Garnish: with toasted sesame seeds

Use scissors and cut the dandelions into small pieces, place in salad bowl along with apples and scallions (variation: ½ cup sliced water chestnuts can be added)
In a small bowl, combine the dressing ingredients and whisk until smooth.
Pour the dressing over the dandelions. Toss well, serve immediately. Garnish with toasted sesame seeds.

"Taste the Freshness"

Hot Dandelion Salad

1 clove of garlic, peeled and slivered
¼ cup of olive oil
3 ½ to 4 cups dandelion, washed, drained and scissor cut into bite-sized pieces
1 cup of sliced raw mushrooms
6 slices of bacon or leftover chicken or turkey
2 green onions, finely chopped
¼ cup of vinegar
¼ tsp. sea salt
Pepper

Let garlic stand in olive oil for 1 hour. Discard garlic. Toss dandelion greens and mushrooms in a bowl and refrigerate.
Fry bacon until crisp, remove from pan and crumble. Reserve 1 tbsp. of fat or a healthier choice would be to add 1 tbsp. of olive oil. Stir in onions and sauté for 2 to 3 minutes. Add garlic flavored oil, vinegar, sea salt and pepper and bring to a boil.
Toss with dandelion and mushrooms. Sprinkle with bacon, or any leftover meat and hard boiled eggs sliced. Serves 4 to 6

Try this as a variation:

Dandelion Salad Dressing

⅓ cup olive oil
¼ cup vinegar
¼ tsp. Tabasco sauce
¼ tsp. dry mustard
½ tsp. sea salt
1 clove garlic, crushed

Mix ingredients well. Store dressing in the fridge.

Eat & Live Better

Dandelion Health Salad for One

1 bunch of dandelion leaves
2 - 3 small red potatoes
1 tbsp. olive oil
1 - 2 tsp. lemon juice
Sea salt and pepper to taste

Boil potatoes before hand and chill. Wash and dry dandelion leaves well. Mix dandelion and chilled potatoes (cut into large chunks) in a large bowl. Add the oil and squeeze half a lemon on top. (Use amount of oil according to your own taste; the dressing should coat the salad lightly), sea salt and pepper to taste and toss well. Serve with slices of whole grain bread on the side.

Add equal amounts for extra servings. Bon Appetite

He provides for the Birds, why would He not for us?

Dandelion and Watercress Salad

3 cups dandelion leaves
1 bunch, 2cups watercress
2 hardboiled eggs, chopped
4 slices of turkey, grilled until crisp

For dressing:
4 tbsp. dry sherry
3 tbsp. olive oil
3 tbsp. wine vinegar
1 tsp. lemon juice
Sea salt and pepper

Wash dandelion and watercress leaves. Dry carefully in tea towel.
To make dressing, whisk all the ingredients together in a bowl, using fork season salad dressing with sea salt and pepper to your liking.
To make salad, cut dandelion into bit size pieces and place in salad bowl with watercress leaves. Pour dressing over salad and toss lightly. Garnish with chopped eggs and crisp bacon. For a healthier version, instead of bacon, use cooked turkey or chicken.

Dandelions are very organic, if untouched by human applied poisons.

Turkey - Tomato Dandelion Salad

8 cups cut fresh dandelion greens
12 cherry tomatoes, halved
½ cup turkey leftovers or bacon or both
¼ cup julienned red onion

Creamy Oregano Dressing

1 cup low fat yogurt
1-2 tbsp. white vinegar
2 tsp. dried oregano
Sea salt and pepper to taste

In large bowl, combine dandelion, tomatoes, turkey and onion. In small bowl, whisk dressing ingredients until smooth.
Serve dressing with salad. Enjoy.

Dandelions are shown to lower and normalize elevated blood sugar. Imagine what this means for diabetics.

Dandelion Turkey-Bacon Salad

2 tbsp. croutons
3 ½ cups cut dandelion greens, reserve ½ cup
3 hardboiled eggs, coarsely chopped
½ cup shaved Parmesan cheese
6 turkey bacon slices, cooked and crumbled

Dandelion Dressing:
½ cup reserved dandelion greens
2 slices of turkey-bacon, cooked crisp and crumbled
⅓ cup buttermilk
¼ cup olive oil
2 tbsp. white wine vinegar
2 tbsp. chopped fresh parsley
1 tbsp. Dijon mustard
1 clove garlic, halved
2 tsp. sugar
¼ tsp. pepper

Place first 5 ingredients in large bowl. Toss.

Dandelion Dressing:
Process all 10 ingredients in food processor until smooth. Drizzle over salad.
Enjoy!

Think before you yank this liver loving herb!

Raspberry Dandelion Salad

4 cups of dandelions
1 cup raspberries
¼ cup each sliced red onion
¼ cup sliced cucumber

Toss together above ingredients.
Dress with ½ cup raspberry vinaigrette dressing.

Makes 4 servings

In this modern toxic-rich life we live, some toxins can be avoided (think cigarettes and artificial preservatives) and some we cannot (think air pollution). Once they enter the body, the liver & kidney are responsible to see it gets the bad out and not left hanging around our circulatory system. Dandelion supports and backs up these systems.

Dandelion Diet Salad

4 cups of young dandelion leaves
4 slices of bacon or use approx. same amount of leftover meat
2 tbsp. sugar
¼ tsp. of powdered mustard
3 tbsp. of cider vinegar
Sea salt and pepper to taste
3 hard cooked eggs, sliced
Olive oil

Wash the dandelion leaves thoroughly, sissor cut, pat or spin dry. Fry the bacon until crisp, remove it from the pan or set aside any leftover meat you have. Add the sugar, mustard, and vinegar to the bacon fat or olive oil. Stir until the sugar is dissolved. Add sea salt and pepper remove from the heat, add the dandelion leaves, and stir to coat evenly. Put the leaves in a bowl. Sprinkle with crumbled bacon or leftover meat and decorate with hard cooked eggs. Serves 4.

Mind Body Connection
True because serotonin is produced in the large intestine and transported to your brain for mood enhancement.

Summer Dandelion Salad for One

1 cup fresh parsley, stemmed
2 Romaine leaves torn and a hand full of cut up dandelion
½ garlic clove, minced
2 tbsp. olive oil
1 tbsp. white vinegar
1 tbsp. grated parmesan

Wash and dry the parsley, lettuce and dandelion. Then stem the parsley and cut or tear the lettuce and dandelion into small pieces, and place them in a bowl. Combine olive oil vinegar and some sea salt and pepper. One hour before eating your salad pour dressing over the greens, add the parmesan, and toss. Cover and chill.

Recent research has shown dandelion roots have a less toxic but potent effect towards Cancer elimination.

Greek Style Dandelion Salad

4 cups dandelion greens
1 pint cherry tomatoes, halved
1 cup mushrooms, sliced
½ cup black olives, sliced
½ cup crushed walnuts
½ cup feta cheese, crumbled
1 cup cucumber, peeled and sliced

Toss well and serve with vinegar dressing

Vinegar Dressing

1/2 cup vegetable or olive oil
½ cup red wine vinegar
¼ cup lemon juice
1 tbsp. parsley
¼ tsp. pepper
¼ tsp. oregano
1 tsp. garlic, minced

Mix all ingredients well, store in fridge in an air-tight container.

Dandelions reduce free radical damage

Dandelion Crouton Salad

2 red peppers, quartered
2 tbsp. melted butter and/or olive oil
1 tbsp. basil pesto
14 baguette bread slices, cut ¼ inch thick
4 cups torn dandelion greens, lightly packed
¼ cup Parmesan cheese

Feta Dressing:
3 tbsp. olive oil
3 tbsp. crumbled Feta cheese
1 tbsp. balsamic vinegar
¼ tsp. pepper
1 tsp. thyme

Arrange red pepper, skin-side, on ungreased baking sheet, 6 inches from heat. Broil for 10-15 minutes, rearranging as necessary, until skin is blistered and blackened. Remove to medium bowl. Cover with foil wrap. Let sweat for 15 minutes until cool enough to handle. Remove and discard skin. Cut into strips. Put into large bowl.

Croutons:
Combine melted butter and/or olive oil and pesto in small bowl. Spread on both sides of each bread slice. Place on lightly greased baking sheet. Bake at 350°F for 5 minutes per side until golden and crisp, cut into cubes as croutons.
Add croutons, dandelion greens and parmesan cheese to red pepper. Toss.

Feta Dressing:
Process all 5 ingredients in blender until smooth spoon over salad.

"Advice on Dandelions: If you can't beat them, eat them."
Dr. James Duke

Dandelion and Chicken Salad with Vinaigrette

Makes 4 servings

8 boneless skinless chicken thighs
Pinch sea salt and pepper
3 cups dandelion
½ cup sliced radishes

Miso Vinaigrette:
2 tbsp. Miso paste
2 tbsp. water
1 tbsp. granulated sugar
or other natural sweetener 1 ½ tsp.
each rice vinegar and olive oil
1 tsp. soy sauce or non-fermenting soy sauce
1 tsp. sesame oil
½ tsp. minced gingerroot

Trim any fat from chicken; sprinkle with sea salt and pepper. Place on greased grill over medium-high heat; close lid and grill, turning once, until lightly marked and juices run clear when chicken is pierced, about 12 minutes.

Miso Vinaigrette:
Meanwhile, in a large bowl, whisk together Miso paste, water, sugar, vinegar, olive oil, soy sauce, sesame oil and ginger.

Slice chicken; add to vinaigrette. Add dandelion and radishes; toss to coat.

Variation: <u>Dandelion and chicken salad with ginger vinaigrette</u>

In small bowl, whisk together 3 tbsp. rice vinegar; 2 tbsp. olive oil; and ½ tsp. each granulated sugar and minced gingerroot. Makes ¼ cup

Enjoy!

Think of them as medicine, not lawn wreckers

Dandelion and Smoked Herring Salad

2 cups dandelion greens
2 oz. lean salt pork with rind removed, blanched in boiling water for 5 mins, drained & diced
1 tbsp. butter
3 or 4 eggs, hard boiled and finely chopped
½ cup vinaigrette
1 pickled herring, skinned, fillet and diced
1 tsp. prepared mustard
Small crusts of bread, rubbed with garlic

Fry salt pork in butter over low heat. Meanwhile, mix eggs with vinaigrette in salad bowl and adjust seasonings to taste.
When the salt pork is golden, add dandelion greens to vinaigrette and toss. Immediately add pork with their fat and the herring to dandelions.
Toss again and serve with bread

The stem of the dandelion leaf is textured, stringy like, celery it balls up like a mini pot scratcher, to clean through our small intestine.

Dandelion Taco Salad

1 lb. ground beef
¼ cup chopped onion
1 ½ tsp. chili pepper
1 clove garlic, minced
½ tsp. pepper
4 cups torn lettuce
2 cups cut fresh dandelion greens
2 cups diced cucumber
1 cup chopped red pepper
6 tbsp. low fat yogurt
2 ½ tbsp. of salsa
1 cup taco chips crumbled
1 ½ cups grated cheddar cheese

Fry first 5 ingredients in large pan on medium-high for 5-10 mins until ground beef is no longer pink. Set aside.
Put next 4 ingredients in large bowl. Toss.
Combine low fat yogurt and salsa in bowl. Add to lettuce mixture. Toss. Divide and arrange dandelion mixture on 4 plates. Divide and spoon beef mixture over each.
Sprinkle taco chips and cheese over top of each.

Dandelion recipes, that include essential minerals from the earth, for a more natural detox on our systems

Dandelion and Turkey Shank Salad

2 cups dandelion greens, stems removed
3 ½ oz. lean turkey shank and cut into strips
1 tbsp. olive oil
1 small heel of dry bread
1 garlic clove, cut in half
Pepper
3 tbsp. wine vinegar
2 eggs, hard-boiled and quartered

In skillet over medium heat, lightly brown turkey shank in oil.
Pour boiling water into a salad bowl to heat it; discard water and wipe bowl dry.
Add dandelion, bread rubbed with the garlic, and pepper to taste.
Throw hot cut turkey shank and its oil it was cooked in into a salad bowl. In same frying pan, bring vinegar to a boil over high heat. Pour vinegar over salad and toss immediately.
Garnish with hard boiled eggs and serve at once.
Enjoy.

Dandelions have been around since the invention of Man, thank God.

Warm Dandelion Country Salad

8 oz. slab of bacon, rind removed, cut into ½ inch diced or use any leftover meat
¼ cup balsamic vinegar
1½ tbsp. Dijon mustard
2 tbsp. of honey
3 tbsp. olive oil
Sea salt and pepper to taste
8 cups of tender dandelion leaves, rinsed and dried
3 oz. goat cheese, crumbled

Fry bacon pieces in skillet until crisp. Remove with a slotted spoon and drain on paper towel. Pour all but ⅓ cup of bacon fat from skillet. Whisk in vinegar, mustard and honey, and then add olive oil, season with sea salt and pepper.
Keep warm.
Toss dandelion leaves with cheese and bacon in salad bowl.
Pour warm dressing over salad and toss to coat.
Serve at once.

A more healthful version is to use any leftover meat and more olive oil, not bacon fat.

Signs, signs everywhere there are signs of dandelions.

Dandelion Floret Salad

4 cups of cut dandelion greens
2 cups torn iceberg lettuce
1 ½ cups broccoli florets
1 ¼ cups cauliflower
1 cup chow mein noodles
8 bacon strips, cooked and crumbled or any leftover turkey or chicken
2 hardboiled eggs, sliced
2 green onions, finely chopped
3 fresh mushrooms, thinly sliced
3 radishes, sliced

Dressing:
1 cup vegetable oil
¾ cup sugar
⅓ cup cider vinegar
¼ cup chopped onion
1 tsp. sea salt
1 tsp. Worcestershire sauce

In salad bowl, toss first 10 ingredients. Place dressing ingredients in a blender. Process until combined. Serve with salad.

Eating healthy is for your own good!

Peachy Dande Tossed Salad

¼ cup orange juice
2 tbsp. cider vinegar
2 tbsp. plain yogurt
1 tbsp. grated orange rind
2 tsp. sugar (optional) or natural sweetener
½ tsp. garlic powder, sea salt
¼ tsp. pepper
½ cup olive oil
8 cups cut dandelion and Romaine lettuce
4 medium peaches, peeled and sliced
½ cup leftover chicken or turkey

In blender, combine first 8 ingredients. While processing, gradually add oil in a steady stream. Process until sugar is dissolved.
In salad bowl, combine dandelion, lettuce, peaches and leftover turkey or chicken. Drizzle with dressing; toss to coat. Serve immediately.

*A study is being done using dandelions,
in Western Ontario, on people with leukemia*

Dandelion and Apricot Salad

2 cups dandelion greens, lightly packed
2 heads of Belgian endive, leaves separated
½ cup chopped dried apricot
⅓ cup sunflower seeds, toasted

Dressing of Herbs and Pepper:
3 tbsp. olive oil
2 tbsp. chopped fresh chives
2 tbsp. chopped fresh parsley
1 tbsp. white wine vinegar
1 tbsp. whole green peppercorns in brine, drained and finely chopped
½ tsp. paprika
¼ tsp. sea salt

Put first 5 ingredients in bowl. Toss.

Dressing of Herbs and Pepper:
Combine all 7 ingredients in jar with tight fitting lid. Shake well. Drizzle over salad. Toss.

Detox from the Earth

Toffee Nut and Dandelion Salad

½ cup slivered almonds, toasted
½ cup sugar
¼ cup water

5 cups dandelion greens, lightly packed
10 oz. can of mandarin orange segments, drained and 3 tbsp. juice reserved

"Low-Fat" Yogurt Dressing
¼ cup low fat yogurt
Reserved mandarin orange juice
1 tbsp. white wine vinegar
2 tsp. grainy mustard
⅛ tsp. sea salt

Arrange almonds in single layer, just touching, on light greased baking sheet.
Put sugar and water into small saucepan. Heat and stir on low until sugar is dissolved. Boil on medium high for about 10 mins, without stirring, until mixture is golden brown. Drizzle over almonds. Let stand for about 20 mins until cool and hard. Chop coarsely.
Put dandelion and orange segments into large bowl. Toss.

Low Fat Yogurt Dressing: Combine all 5 ingredients in jar with tight fitting lid. Shake well. Drizzle over salad. Add almonds. Toss.

Make Dandelions your daily diet

Exotic Dandelion Salad

Dressing:
½ cup olive oil
¼ cup sugar (organic)
2 tbsp. sesame seeds
1 tbsp. sliced green onion
½ tsp. paprika
¼ tsp. Worcestershire sauce
1 ½ tsp. poppy seeds
¼ cup apple cider vinegar
1 ½ tsp. poppy seeds

3 cups dandelion greens
1 medium kiwifruit, sliced
1 cup sliced strawberries
½ medium mango, diced
½ medium papaya, seeded and diced

Dressing: Process first 7 ingredients in blender for 5 sec. With motor running, slowly add vinegar through hole in lid.
Put remaining 5 ingredients into large bowl. Drizzle with dressing, sprinkle in poppy seeds. Toss.

It's been shown to stop tumor formation and growths.

Dandelion and Blueberry Salad

2 cups dandelion greens
1 cup blueberries
1 ½ cups pecans, toasted and coarsely chopped
6 bacon slices, cooked crisp and crumbled; healthier version would be without bacon or try turkey bacon

Parmesan Dressing
¼ cup olive oil
3 tbsp. grated Parmesan cheese
2 tbsp. white wine vinegar
1 tsp. organic sugar
¼ tsp. coarsely ground pepper

Put first 4 ingredients into bowl. Toss.

Parmesan Dressing: Process all 5 ingredients in blender until smooth. Drizzle over salad. Toss.

Dandelion has been shown to stimulate cancer-fighting immune cells

Grape Dandelion Salad

4 cups dandelion greens, lightly packed
1 cup sliced fresh strawberries
½ cup seedless green grapes, halved
½ cup seedless red grapes, halved
¼ cup sunflower seeds, toasted

Poppy Seed Dressing
2 tbsp. olive oil
2 tbsp. balsamic vinegar
1 tbsp. maple syrup,
1 tbsp. poppy seeds
¼ tsp. sea salt

Arrange dandelion greens on 4 individual plates.
Top with strawberries, grapes and sunflower seeds.

Poppy Seed dressing: Combine all 5 ingredients in jar with tight fitting lid. Shake well and drizzle over salad.

When all the trees have been cut down, when all the animals have been hunted, when all the waters are polluted, when all the air is unsafe to breathe, only then will you discover you can't eat money.
Cree Prophecy

Strawberry-Dandelion Salad

Prep: 10 minutes
Cooking time: 5 minutes
Makes 4 to 8 servings, and ⅔ cup dressing

⅓ cup pecan pieces, toasted
1 pint strawberries, stems removed
8 cups cut up dandelions and baby spinach mixed half and half
2 green onions, thinly sliced
¼ cup bottle blue cheese dressing
¼ cup crumbled blue cheese or Stilton (optional)

Place pecans in a small, ungreased frying pan over medium heat. Stir often until fragrant, 5 to 7 minutes. Or spread nuts in a pie plate and toast in center of a preheated 350°F oven, stirring occasionally, 5 to 10 minutes. Let cool.

Slice three-quarters of strawberries into quarters and place in a large salad bowl. Add Dandelions onions and pecans. Toss until evenly mixed. Coarsely chop remaining berries and place in bowl of a food processor. Add dressing, then whirl just until blended, leaving some berries chunky. Dressing will be quite thick. Just before serving, pour dressing over salad and toss into evenly coat. Crumble cheese over top.

Eat Local Eat Colorful

Fruit and Honey Dandelion Salad

8 cups dandelion cut up
2 cups cantaloupe balls
1 ½ cups of halved strawberries
1 cup blackberries
¼ cup raspberry jam
¼ cup vinegar
2 tbsp. honey
2 tbsp. olive oil
¼ cup chopped macadamia nuts

Combine dandelions, cantaloupe, strawberries and blackberries in a large bowl and toss gently.
Combine the jam, vinegar, honey and olive oil in a small bowl; stir well with a whisk. Drizzle the dressing over the dandelion mixture and toss gently to coat. Sprinkle with chopped macadamia nuts.

There are nations at stake here. Get off the sugar.

Dandelion, Pear and Bacon Salad with Blue Cheese Dressing

⅓ cup sour cream
½ cup low fat yogurt
½ tsp. Worcestershire sauce
Sea salt and pepper to taste
2 oz. blue cheese, crumbled
6 cups cut dandelion greens
3 pears, peeled, halved, sliced thinly
6 slices cooked bacon, crumbled or leftover meat (better choice)
1 cup walnuts

In medium bowl, combine sour cream, low fat yogurt, Worcestershire sauce, sea salt, pepper and blue cheese.
Set aside.
To serve, place dandelion, pear slices, meat and walnuts in a large bowl and toss gently with dressing.

Greens are vital!

Dandelion and Pear Salad with Feta

1 medium pear cored
2 tbsp. of lemon juice
4 cups of chopped dandelions
1 ½ cups of crumbled feta cheese
¼ cup of chopped walnuts
¼ cup of olive oil
3 tbsp. of organic brown sugar

In a medium bowl coat the pear with lemon juice to keep from browning.
This is a four serving salad. Arrange the dandelions, pears, feta and walnuts evenly proportioned on individual plates.

Salad Dressing: In a small bowl, whisk together olive oil, vinegar and brown sugar.
Drizzle the dressing evenly on top.

Dandelions are a widely accepted diuretic that don't deplete potassium and can be safely consumed in frequent doses

Strawberry and Dandelion Salad

1 lb. fresh strawberries
3 ½ to 4 cups fresh dandelion

Dressing:
1 egg
¼ cup organic sugar or other natural sweetener
1 tbsp. Dijon mustard
⅔ cup red wine
½ tsp. sea salt
3 tbsp. grated yellow onion and juice
2 cups olive oil
3 tbsp. poppy seeds

Blend the first six ingredients of the Dressing. Add the olive oil slowly, blending until incorporated. Add the poppy seeds.

Pour dressing over dandelion and strawberries, enjoy.

Nature's generosity brings dandelions for our cleansing and good health.

Cranberry Dandelion Salad

3 cups of dandelions
½ cup raisins or dried cranberries
Red onion slices

Dressing
4 slices bacon crumbled, bacon optional
½ cup honey
½ cup lime juice
2 tbsp. Dijon mustard

Wash and dry, and cut up dandelions. Divide among 4 salad plates. Top each with 2 tbsp. cranberries, raisins, and red onion slices.

Combine dressing ingredients in small glass mixing bowl using wire whisk.
Heat dressing in microwave on high, for 1 minute.
Pour dressing over salad.

If it isn't real food, don't eat it!

Cranberry and Dandelion Salad

1 tbsp. olive oil
¾ cup almonds slivered
3 ½ to 4 cups dandelion
1 cup dried cranberries

Dressing
2 tbsp. toasted sesame seeds
1 tbsp. poppy seeds
½ cup white organic sugar
2 tsp. minced onion
¼ tsp. paprika
¼ cup white wine vinegar
¼ cup cider vinegar
¼ cup olive oil

In a saucepan, warm 1 tbsp. olive oil over med. heat. Cook and stir almonds in olive oil until lightly toasted. Remove from heat. Let cool.
In a large bowl, combine the dandelion with the toasted almonds and cranberries.
In a med. bowl, whisk together the sesame seeds, poppy seeds, sugar, onion, paprika, white wine vinegar, cider vinegar, and olive oil. Toss with dandelion just before serving.

Eating dandelions is not the same as eating sub-standard nutrition from groceries provided by food manufacturers.

Dandelion and Fruit Salad with a Tasty Dressing

4 slices of bacon or ½ cup of cooked chicken
4 cups of torn dandelion
1 cup of mandarin orange segments, drained and chopped
½ cup sliced onion
1 cup olive oil
3 tbsp. lemon juice
1 tsp. sea salt
2 tsp. paprika
1 small onion, chopped
1 tsp. dry mustard
1 clove garlic, crushed

Fry bacon until crisp, drain and crumble or pre-cooked chicken meat. Combine with dandelion, mandarin orange segments and sliced onion. To make dressing, combine remaining ingredients, refrigerate and shake vigorously before using. Serves 6 to 8

A cheerful heart is good medicine, but a downcast spirit dries the bones
-Proverbs 17:22

Dandelions, Mango and Orange Salad

If one can find mangoes, this is a delicious and exotic salad, especially in the winter when it could conjure thoughts of a warm tropical summer day.

3 ½ to 4 cups fresh dandelion
2 navel oranges
2 mangoes
6 strips of bacon or healthy choice, use ½ cup of cooked chicken

Dressing:
½ tsp. sea salt and pepper
1 tbsp. Dijon mustard
2 tbsp. white wine vinegar
1 tsp. lemon juice
⅔ cup olive oil
1 small diced onion

Wash, dry, and cut dandelion. Peel and section oranges. Peel mangoes, remove pits, and cut unto bit-sized strips. Cook bacon until crispy, drain then crumble or use leftover cooked chicken (½ cup).

For the dressing, combine onion, sea salt, pepper, dijon mustard, vinegar and lemon juice in a small bowl. Mix well, and then beat in the olive oil very slowly. Continue beating until dressing thickens. Pour over dandelion, oranges, mangoes and bacon (or chicken), toss. Let stand for 10 minutes. Serves 6

We're taught sweet is good & bitter is bad but it's really the other way round.

Crunchy Dandelion Salad

6 cups dandelion greens, lightly packed
2 cups halved cherry tomatoes
8 oz. can of sliced water chestnuts, drained
8 slices bacon slices, cooked crisp and crumbled, or a healthier choice of meat would be to use ¾ cup of cooked chicken or turkey

Green Onion Dressing
3 tbsp. olive oil
⅓ cup chopped green onion
1 clove garlic, minced
2 tbsp. balsamic vinegar
1 tsp. Worcestershire sauce
1 tsp. brown sugar, packed or equivalent natural sweetener
2 cups dry chow mein noodles

Put first 4 ingredients into large bowl. Toss.

Green Onion Dressing: Heat olive oil in small frying pan on medium low. Add green onion and garlic. Cook for about 5 mins until onion is soft.
Process onion mixture, vinegar, Worcestershire sauce and brown sugar in blender until smooth. Drizzle over salad. Top with chow mein noodles.

Dandelion has a History, Edible green leaves found on the ground by hunters and gatherers, gardeners and people who just need to eat!

Dandelion & Sprout Salad with Honey Dressing

3 cups dandelion cut into bite size pieces
1 cup alfalfa sprouts
1 cup sliced mushrooms
½ cup feta cheese chunks
2 tbsp. poppy seeds

Honey Dressing:
½ cup liquid honey
¼ cup hot water
¼ cup lemon juice
¼ cup olive oil
¼ tsp. sea salt
¼ ground ginger
Dash ground cloves

For honey dressing, blend ingredients in a shaker or hand mixer. Wash and spin dandelion leaves and scissor cut into large bowl. Blend with mushrooms, feta cheese and poppy seeds. Pour the dressing over top of the dandelion mixture.

Our animal instinct to survive; Included dandelions.

Dandelion and Flower Salad

2 cups of young dandelion leaves
2 cups of young leaves from romaine or spinach or any combination
½ cup walnut pieces
1 cup diced chicken
¼ cup of canned crushed pineapple
¼ cup plus 2 tbsp. of low fat yogurt
½ tsp. of pepper
A few violets, nasturtiums, or roses for garnish

Wash the greens, pat or spin-dry. Tear them into bite size pieces and mix them in a large bowl. Add the walnuts, chicken and pineapple; toss. Mix in the low fat yogurt and pepper. Decorate each serving with flowers. Serves 4

This recipe is also good with diced ham and grated cheese. Substituted for the chicken and pineapple; use an unseasoned oil and vinegar dressing instead of low fat yogurt.

Always do what you can, because once you at least do what you can, no matter how seemingly insignificant, everything changes.

Dandelion Salad with Pecan Dressing

Salad:
6 cups dandelion greens, washed and torn into bite size pieces
2 oranges cut into segments
4 fresh mushrooms, thinly sliced
Thinly sliced red onion to taste
½ cup toasted pecans

Dressing:
2 tbsp. pecans
1 clove garlic
¼ tsp. sea salt and sugar
Ground pepper to taste
1 tbsp. balsamic and white vinegar, orange juice
⅓ cup olive oil

Drop garlic into feed tube of running food processor. When garlic is minced, add 2 tbsp. pecans and seasoning, pulse until pecans are finely chopped. Add vinegars. Pulse, to blend with machine running slowly pour oil through the tube.
Taste and adjust seasonings.
Pour over salad.

Are you confused about potions, pills, prescriptions and remedies of the 1900's? Well dandelions have been around longer.

Dandegreen Soups

Pumpkin-Dandelion Soup

Prepare in advance:

1 large handful Dandelion greens: Chop leaves into bite-sized pieces. Cook in boiling water until tender. Pour off water and taste. If they seem too bitter for your taste, boil again and strain.

1 small pumpkin: Bake whole pumpkin on baking sheet at 350° for 1 hour or until completely soft, so that you can put a fork or knife easily through it. Let cool. Cut in half and discard seeds. Rind will peel easily.

1 medium to large onion, chopped
6 cloves garlic, minced
2 Tbsp. butter or olive oil
6 cups water
4 cups mashed pumpkin, prepared as above
1 cup heavy cream
½ tsp nutmeg
1½ tsp salt

1. Sauté onion and garlic in oil or butter in a heavy-bottomed soup pot.
2. Add 6 cups water
3. Add dandelion greens and pureed pumpkin to soup. Stir well.
4. Add salt. Cook at a gentle simmer for 30 minutes.
5. Just before serving add 1 cup heavy cream and ½ tsp nutmeg.

Thanks to Rose Barlow's Original Prodigal Gardens Website

A journey of a thousand miles must begin with a single step.

Dandelion and Thai Noodle Soup

Makes 4 servings

½ oz. dried shiitake mushrooms
1 tsp. olive oil
½ cup thinly sliced shallots
2 Thai chilies, seeded and finely minced
1 one-inch piece fresh ginger, finely chopped
1 lemon grass stalk
3 kafir lime leaves
2 tbsp. fish sauce
1 tsp. granulated sugar
¾ cup chopped cooked turkey
5 cups turkey stock
2 vermicelli noodle bundles (3 oz. in total)
1 ½ cups chopped baby bok choy and scissor cut dandelion greens

Soak mushrooms on boiling water for 10 minutes to re-hydrate. Drain and squeeze to remove excess water. Roughly chop if mushrooms are large.

In a medium-sized pot, sauté, mushrooms, shallots, chilies and ginger in olive oil over medium heat.

Remove outer hard layer from lemon grass then cut stalk in half. Braise the thick end with remaining ingredients, except noodles, to pot and bring to boil. Reduce heat to simmer, add noodles and cook until tender.

Remove kafir lime leaves and lemongrass and add chopped greens to serve.

Natural Health…………..

Dandelion Soup

Brown 2 cloves of crushed garlic with chopped onion in olive oil.

2 cups of water
Handful of parsley
3 cups of dandelions

-Bring to a boil cook for 3 to 4 minutes.
-Season it with sea salt and pepper, put in blender.
-Reheat and serve.

Suggestion:
-Eat with a sesame and rye cracker which you could use as a dip or pâté, great on top of cheesecake. (My daughter, Megan even liked it – she said green topping looks good at Christmas a nice change from the most popular red topping of cherry cheese cake!)
-Try the dandelion soup, blended with 1 cooked carrot.
-For a different taste try with basil or apple sauce.
-Dandelion soup makes a great addition to many soups and sauces
Try freezing some in ice cube trays then put frozen cubes in freezer bags for later use.
(e.g. spaghetti sauce, stir fry's, casseroles).

Enjoy!

Eat good,
Feel good,
Look good,
Do good.

Mushroom Tomato Dandelion Pasta Soup

2 tbsp. butter or olive oil
1 medium onion, chopped
2 cups sliced mushrooms
1 19 oz. can stewed tomatoes
1 10 oz. can chicken broth
1 can water
½ tsp. dried tarragon or basil
¾ cup macaroni
2 cups dandelion, cut into bite size pieces
1 ¼ cups shredded Swiss cheese

Melt butter or olive oil, sauté onion, and mushrooms for 2 mins.
Add tomatoes, broth, water, and spices.
Bring to a boil.
Stir in pasta. Reduce heat and simmer for 10 mins. or until pasta is tender, stirring occasionally
Stir in dandelions, heat for 1 min or just until wilted.
Serve immediately in bowls.
Sprinkle with cheese

Eating green is a logical necessity, not a sharpened political correctness lets show the children tomorrow how to grow up green.

Dandelion and Spinach Soup

6 cups of chicken stock
3 cups of chopped dandelion greens
3 cups of chopped spinach
3 green onions, chopped
1 clove garlic, crushed, sea salt and pepper, nutmeg
2 hard-cooked eggs, chopped

Heat chicken stock and add dandelion greens. Cook for 3 minutes, and then add spinach, onions, garlic and sea salt and pepper. Cook until greens are tender for 5 minutes. Serve with nutmeg and eggs. Serves 6

Special thanks to Mary Elizabeth Marshall, Thunder Bay, ON

Sharing the journey armed with new information

Spring Vegetable Soup and Fresh Parsley

½ cup vegetable stock or apple juice
2 cloves of garlic
2 stalks of celery chopped
1 medium carrot chopped
1 small onion chopped
1 small red bell pepper chopped
1 can diced tomatoes
1 medium potato, peeled and diced
5 cups vegetable stock
½ teaspoon black pepper
½ teaspoon dried thyme
OR
1 tablespoon of chopped fresh thyme
½ teaspoon of sea salt
½ cup of chopped fresh parsley
½ cup fresh chopped or scissor cut dandelion

Hint: For a different flavor replace fresh parsley with fresh coriander.

- In the pot, heat vegetable stock or apple juice on medium heat and gently sauté garlic, celery, carrot, onion and red bell pepper for about 3-4 minutes.
- Add all the other ingredients, except parsley and dandelion and bring the mixture to a boil on high heat. Reduce the heat to medium and simmer for 12 to 15 minutes.
- Add dandelions for 2 - 3 minutes and then add parsley and serve immediately.

Makes 6 servings prep time 10 min. Cook time – 15 minutes in one large pot.

Good food, good reason

Dandelion Soup with Dill & Lemon

3 tbsp. butter or olive oil
2 onions, chopped
3 ½ to 4 cups dandelions, washed & stems removed
2 cups of peas
1 cup of cooked rice
2 tbsp. chopped dill
4 cups of chicken stock
Sea salt and pepper to taste
Nutmeg to taste
Grated peel of ½ lemon
1 cup of heavy cream
½ cup of low fat yogurt
Chopped dill

Serve this soup hot or chilled – it tastes dande good either way.
Melt butter or olive oil and sauté onions until tender. Add rice and peas and toss, and then add dill and chicken stock. Bring to a boil stir in sea salt and pepper, nutmeg, and lemon peel. Reduced heat, cover and simmer for 20 minutes or until rice is tender. Add dandelions and cook, stiring till it wilts. Puree, in batches, in blender or food processor. Stir in cream just before serving. Serve with a dollop of low fat yogurt and dill.

Flush away toxins with dandelions for better health

Dandelion Green (cold soup)

This is a light meal all by itself. Serve with a green salad and fresh bread.

2 tbsp. butter or olive oil
5 small leeks, white part only
6 cups of chicken stock
2 medium baking potatoes, peeled & diced
4 cups of fresh dandelion leaves
1 cup heavy cream
Sea salt and pepper

Heat butter or olive oil and gently sauté leeks for 10 minutes, then add chicken stock and potatoes and simmer until potatoes are tender – about 20 minutes. Add dandelion and simmer 5 minutes longer. Puree soup, leaving flecks of green, and chill for at least 3 hours. Add cream and season to taste with sea salt and pepper. Garnish with springs of dandelions or parsley.
Serves 6

Living the Green life

Chilled Cream of Dandelion Soup

8 cups of dandelions
½ cup butter or olive oil
2 onions, chopped
7 ½ cups chicken stock
½ tsp. sea salt and pepper
1 ½ tbsp. lemon juice
2 bay leaves
¼ cup flour
⅛ cup light cream
Croutons and grated cheese

Wash and drain dandelions. In pan, melt half of the butter or olive oil and sauté onions until soft but not colored. Add dandelions and sauté 5 mins, stirring constantly. Add stock, sea salt, pepper, lemon juice and bay leaves. Bring to a boil. Simmer 5 mins. Adjust seasoning. Turn into a bowl and chill.
Just before serving, pour into soup cup and add a little cream to each serving. Sprinkle cheese on croutons on baking sheet and melt under hot broiler. Serve with soup.

"Wellness", herbs balance health

Garden Dandelion Soup

1 tbsp. butter or olive oil
3 cloves garlic, minced
2 each, carrots and stalks celery, diced
1 diced onion
¾ tsp. dried rosemary or thyme
2 cups vegetable or chicken stock
2 potatoes cut into cubes
2 tomatoes, chopped
2 tbsp. tomato paste
3 tbsp. flour
3 cups milk
1 cup finely chopped broccoli or peas
2 cups dandelion greens
Sea salt

In large pot, melt butter or olive oil over medium heat; cook garlic, carrots, celery, onions and rosemary, stirring until onions are softened. Stir in vegetable stock and potatoes; bring to a boil over high heat, stirring often. Reduce heat, cover and simmer until potatoes are tender. Stir in tomatoes and tomato paste. Cook covered until tomatoes are softened. Increase heat to medium. Whisk flour into milk, gradually stir into pot. Stir in broccoli or peas. Cook uncovered stirring often until broccoli or peas are tender. Stir in dandelion greens just until wilted. Season to taste, with sea salt and pepper, serve.

From the Ground, Up

Dandelion and Shrimp Soup

1 lb. uncooked shrimp (with shells)
7 cups water
1 cup dry white wine
½ cup chopped onions
½ cup carrots
1 tbsp. olive oil
1 cup chopped onion
4 garlic cloves, minced
1 tbsp. flour
6 cups fresh dandelion greens, coarsely chopped
2 tbsp. chopped fresh parsley
1 tsp. sea salt
1 can of evaporated milk

Peel and devein shrimp, reserving shells and tails. Coarsely chop shrimp. Transfer to medium bowl. Set aside.
Put reserved shells and tails into large pot. Add next 4 ingredients. Stir. Bring to a boil over medium-high heat. Reduce heat to medium. Simmer uncovered for 20 mins, stirring occasionally. Strain through sieve into large bowl.
Discard solids. Set liquid, aside.
Heat olive oil in the same pot on medium. Add second amount of onion. Cook for 5-10 mins, stirring often until softened.
Add garlic. Heat and stir for 1-2 minutes. Add flour. Heat and stir for 1 minute. Slowly add reserved liquid, stirring constantly, until boiling and slightly thickened. Reduce heat to medium-low. Simmer uncovered for 5 mins, stirring occasionally.
Add dandelion, parsley and sea salt. Heat and stir for about 3 mins until dandelion is wilted. Add shrimp and milk. Heat and stir on medium-high for about 2 mins until shrimp turns pink.

Food to survive

Beef and Dandelion Soup

Wash and cut 3 to 4 cups dandelion greens. Drain well.
Boil 6 cups of water and add 2 pkgs. of beef bouillon.
Thinly slice 1 lb. of round steak after marinating it
In, 2 tbsp. of soy sauce, 1 tbsp. cornstarch and pepper to taste.
Add beef to boiling water. Simmer for 5-10 minutes or longer.
Add dandelion greens and simmer until limp.

Hallelujah means a shout of joy!

Dandelions are said to bring "joy" Hallelujah!

Dandelion Tortellini Soup

3 cloves garlic, minced
1 tbsp. butter or olive oil
1 can (48 oz.) chicken or beef broth
1 pkg. (19 oz.) frozen cheese tortellini
3 cups frozen chopped dandelion greens
2 cans (14 ½ oz.) each stewed tomatoes, non-drained, cut into pieces
Grated parmesan cheese

In large saucepan, over medium high heat, cook garlic in butter or olive oil for 1-2 minutes. Add broth and tortellini. Heat to a boil; reduce heat and simmer 10 mins. Add dandelion and tomatoes; simmer 5 minutes longer.
Sprinkle each serving with cheese.

Wart remover
Take the white fluid from the dandelion stem or root and dab on warts.
Apply daily sometimes twice till it disappears.

Dandelion Soup with Lemon and Feta

1 tbsp. olive oil
1 cup sliced leek
2 garlic cloves, minced
1 potato, peeled and diced
4 cups chicken stock
3 cups dandelion greens
Juice of 1 lemon
½ tsp. sea salt, pepper
⅓ cup crumbled feta cheese

Heat olive oil in saucepan. Add leeks, garlic and potato; cook and stir over medium heat, until leeks are tender but not brown.
Stir in stock; cover and cook for 20 mins or until potato is tender. Add dandelion, lemon juice, and sea salt and pepper.
Cover and cook for 10 minutes more.
Transfer solids to food processor. Puree until smooth.
Return to saucepan with liquid and heat until hot. Taste and adjust seasonings.
Spoon heated mixture into warmed soup bowls. Garnish each serving with feta cheese.

Every small step you take helps

Dandelion Soup

-Brown two cloves of crushed garlic in olive oil
 One onion chopped.
-2 cups of water
-Add a handful of parsley
-2 cups of dandelions
-Season with sea salt and pepper and put in a blender to combine.
Pour soup into a sauce pan, heat and Enjoy!

Dandelion soup can be frozen in muffin tins or ice cube trays for additions to bowls of soup for lunch, spaghetti sauces, casseroles, quiches, or meat loafs. The uses are endless to your imagination.
Too bad major soup manufactures wouldn't can, or freeze dry dandelion so to make it available for everyone's use. Hint Hint.

Dandelions are good for all blood types!

Dandelion Smoothie Recipes

Power to the Prostate

½ cup orange juice
¼ cup blueberries
¼ cup seedless red grapes, halved
1 cup fresh or frozen dandelion
1 tbsp. flax seeds
1 tsp. dried skullcap (optional)
1 tsp. lecithin

In blender, combine all ingredients. Process as directed until smooth. Feel the power, enjoy!

Think of food as a prescription you take to feel better. "Know your food".

Dandegreen Gold

⅔ cup carrot juice
⅓ cup apple juice
½ cup chopped fresh or frozen dandelion greens
Half cucumber, peeled and chopped
1 apple, peeled, cored and chopped
2 tsp. chopped fresh basil leaves

In blender, combine carrot juice, apple juice, dandelion, cucumber, apple and basil.
Process until smooth
Enjoy winning gold.

Let food be your medicine

Popeye's Dande Power

½ cup beet or carrot juice
1 cup cooked diced beets
½ cup chopped or frozen dandelion greens
½ cup cooked chopped carrots
1 piece (approx. 1 in.) dandelion root
1 tbsp. blackstrap molasses

In blender, combine all ingredients and process as directed until smooth.

Feel the energy.

Makes one serving

Eat dandelions gain a better sense of well being.

Dandegreen Vegetable Side Dishes

Dandelions in Butter

Wash 4 to 6 cups of dandelions several times in water to remove all grit and strip off coarse stalks. Pack into a saucepan with only the water that clings to the leaves after washing.

Heat gently, turning dandelion occasionally, then bring to a boil and cook gently for 6-8 minutes or until tender.

Drain thoroughly. Chop roughly or puree and reheat with butter or olive oil and sprinkle with sea salt and pepper.

Dandelions:
-may cause you to live longer
-may cause you to feel more relaxed
-may cause sexual enhancement
-may have overall better concentration
-may hurt less
-may sleep better -may you live dande

Lightened "Creamed" Dandelion

Makes: 2 to 3 servings

¼ cup light or regular herbed cream cheese
2 tbsp. milk
2 tsp. lemon juice
Pinch both sea salt and pepper
Pinch nutmeg
1 ½ cups chopped dandelion, cooked drained

1. In skillet or saucepan, whisk together cream cheese, milk, lemon juice, sea salt, pepper and nutmeg over medium-low heat until melted and smooth.
2. Finally add dandelion to cheese mixture and cook, stirring, until blended and hot, about 2 minutes.

Tip: You can multiply this dish as desired.

My message is simple, make dandelions better known for their health benefits, and you and your loved ones could live longer.

Sweet and Sour Dandelion

4 cups dandelion
4 slices bacon, cut into strips
1 tbsp. flour
½ cup water
3 tbsp. cider vinegar
1 ½ tsp. sugar
¼ tsp. sea salt, pepper

Trim dandelion and wash it. Place dandelion into large pot with just a little water and cook, covered for 5 minutes or until it is just limp. Drain and press out as much liquid as you can. Put dandelion into a serving bowl and set in a keep-warm (250°F) oven. While dandelion is heating, cook bacon until crisp. Drain on paper towel, set aside and pour out all but 1 tbsp. of bacon drippings. Or a healthier choice would be to add any leftover meat.
Blend flour into remaining drippings or use 1 tbsp. olive oil, for a healthier choice.
Mix together the water, vinegar, sugar, sea salt, and pepper. Add the mixture slowly to the bacon drippings and flour, blending until smooth and thick. Pour sauce over dandelion. Serve with bacon crumbled, or your choice of leftover meat on top.
That's the healthier choice.

The lion in the dandelion is from the jagged leaves that looked a bit like a lion's tooth

"Creamed" Dandelion Greens

Makes: 2 to 3 servings

¼ cup herbed cream cheese
2 tbsp. milk
2 tsp. lemon juice
Pinch sea salt and pepper
Pinch nutmeg
2 cups chopped dandelion, cooked drained

In skillet or saucepan, wisk together cream cheese, milk, lemon juice, sea salt, pepper and nutmeg over medium-low heat until melted and smooth looking.
Chop dandelion; add to cheese mixture and heat. Stir until blended and hot, about 2 minutes.
Tip: You can multiply this dish as desired for more tasty servings. Serve with any meal anytime of the day. Variations; add frozen green peas and heat through. You could serve over toast.

I'm here to boost your faith in Dandegreen plant power.

Creamed Dandelion

6 to 8 cups of dandelion greens
1 white bread roll, soaked in water
3 tbsp. olive oil
4 tbsp. flour
Milk
2 cloves of garlic, minced
Sea salt

Slice and put dandelion greens in saucepan over brisk heat. Cook until limp and tender. Squeeze liquid out of bread roll; sieve the roll and dandelion together or blend them to a puree in blender. In saucepan, gently heat 3 tbsp. of olive oil, add the garlic and when it is bubbling, add flour to make a paste. Stir until paste changes color to beige. Add dandelion-bread mixture and enough milk to make a thick sauce, stirring all the time until bubbles break the surface. Add sea salt to taste and continue to cook, stirring for a few more minutes.

It's simple but it works for you.

Dandelion and Mixed Greens with Parmesan Crisps

Makes: 8 servings, 1 cup salad and 2 parmesan crisps each.

1 cup grated parmesan cheese
2 tsp. finally chopped fresh rosemary
8 cups baby mixed salad greens with dandelions
½ cup seedless red grapes, halved
½ cup walnut pieces
½ cup sun dried tomato and oregano dressing

1. Preheat oven to 400°F. Mix cheese and rosemary. Place 1 tbsp of cheese on a lightly greased baking sheet, spread slightly to flatten.
2. Repeat with remaining cheese, making 16 crisps total, and allowing 1 inch between each flattened crisp. Bake 5 minutes. Turn crisps over; bake an additional 1 minute or until golden brown. Cool on wire rack.
3. Place 1 cup greens on each of 8 plates. Top with 1 tbsp. grape halves and 1 tbsp. walnuts. Drizzle with 1 tbsp. dressing. Serve each salad with 2 crisps.

There's nothing more rewarding than making a difference in your life or that of your loved ones.

Dandelion on Toast & Blueberry Jam

My grandson suggested, Nanny try this! make your toast, put blueberry jam on top.
Then add your dandelions on top of the jam.
This tastes, really good.
Try other jams, too.

My Granddaughter says she like dandelion, too.
Grandma says: Cut dandelion up small and add it to wilt in your gravy and sauces. Hide it in other dishes too! IT'S VERY GOOD.

Caution: Avoid dandelion if you have gallbladder disease. If you have diabetes, monitor blood sugar levels while using this herb.

Dandelion Spicy Greens

Makes: 6 servings

The Portuguese & Italians love their greens and they appear in many dishes, soups and side dishes. This is a green recipe that complements a pork dish.

2 tbsp. olive oil
1 tbsp. chopped fresh garlic
¼ tsp. chili flakes
4 cups Swiss chard leaves cleaned
4 cups dandelion
4 cups spinach, cleaned
¼ cup water

Heat olive oil in a skillet on medium heat. Add garlic and chili flakes and sauté for 1 minute. Add Swiss chard and cook for 1 minute. Add spinach and dandelion and cook for one minute more.
Add water and simmer for 2 minutes or until chard ribs and dandelion are tender and water has evaporated.

It's all about time and signs, and sign of the times. It's all about signs.

Braised Dandegreens and Garlic

2 cups dandelion greens
4 to 6 cloves of garlic, crushed and peeled
2 tbsp. of olive oil
½ cup of water
Add enough sea salt for taste

Wash the greens very well, because some of them are exceptionally gritty and carelessness at this stage of preparation can result in a less pleasant dining experience. Some greens have leaves that are wider than the rest. Though the wider leaves, it's a good idea to cut them, if you do decide to cut them then cut all them including the stems. Heat the olive oil in a heavy skillet with a lid over medium heat. Add garlic and sauté until it softens. Add cut green leaves, turning them in the oil. The leaves will be voluminous, but they will be reduced in size, substantially by the time they're ready to be eaten. Reduce heat and cook for several minutes. The moisture retained during washing should be all the water the greens need. After several minutes, add ½ cup of water and cover skillet. Check frequently to be sure there is still water, adding a few tablespoons at a time as necessary. Doneness varies from green to green. They should be soft and limp, and almost all of the water should have evaporated. Add sea salt for taste. Serves 2-3

Now my Grandchildren are learning to respect and enjoy the dandelions. They pick them for us.

Dandelion Provincial

8 cups dandelion leaves
1 large onion, sliced
1 clove garlic, minced
Olive oil
Butter
2 eggs, beaten
1 cup grated Parmesan cheese
Sea salt and Pepper

-Wash and scissor cut dandelion. Sauté onion and garlic in olive oil until the onion is transparent. Add dandelion, cover and cook until dandelion is wilted – about 2 minutes. Remove from heat and cool slightly.

-In a baking dish, combine dandelion mixture, beaten eggs and half the cheese. Season, and sprinkle the remaining cheese on top. Dot the dandelion mixture with butter or olive oil and bake for 375°F for 10 to 15 minutes. Serves 6 to 8

Dandelion Rx
Don't like tea, instead use dandelion tincture 1:5
1 teaspoon, three times a day, or take two 500 mg capsules of dried dandelion root three Rx's a day. Or 10 leaves a day for 2 weeks supposed to bring joy.

Wilted Garlic Dandelions

8 cups dandelions
3 cloves garlic, minced
3 tbsp. butter or olive oil
Sea salt and pepper to taste

Clean dandelions in sink full of cold water.
Melt butter or olive oil in large saucepan; add garlic and sauté carefully, do not brown.
Remove dandelions from sink, do not dry.
Place dandelions in saucepan, cover and cook for 5-6 minutes, stirring occasionally until wilted.
Serve as a side dish.

Dandelion leaves in a bath
-cleansing, add an infusion. To infuse add a handful of leaves or flowers in 2 pints of boiling water, then add to bath - its effect is cleansing.

Dandelion on the Side

Lightly, brown 2 tsp of pine nuts in a dry skillet. (shake the pan so they don't burn)
Add 4 cut cups of just washed, damp dandelions.
Add 2 tbsp. raisins.
Cover and cook 2 to 4 mins, just until the dandelion is wilted.

Potential uses:
Kidney and liver disorders
A natural diuretic and digestive aid
Reduces blood pressure
May help prevent iron deficiency, anemia, chronic rheumatism, gout and stiff joints

Italian Dandelions

8 cups of dandelion, well washed and trimmed
3 tbsp. butter
3 tbsp. olive oil
1 clove garlic, chopped
Sea salt to taste
¼ tsp. cayenne pepper or to taste
Coarsely grated parmesan cheese

Cut dandelions into coarse shreds. Plunge into boiling water to cover and parboil thirty seconds. Drain well and place in baking dish.
In skillet heat the butter and olive oil. Add garlic, sea salt and cayenne pepper and cook over low heat five minutes. Combine oil mixture with dandelion and sprinkle with cheese.
Brown the dandelion dish quickly under broiler.

I can't believe if you knew now, how good you could feel, to heal on the inside out.

Sour Cream and Onion Dandelions

8 cups fresh, washed dandelion greens
1 tbsp. butter or olive oil
1 tbsp. flour
½ cup sour cream or low fat yogurt
½ tsp. minced onion
Sea salt and pepper to taste

Cook dandelion, covered, in a small amount of boiling water until just tender. Drain thoroughly and chop. Melt the butter or olive oil and blend the flour. Add sour cream and onion and cook, stirring constantly, until the mixture thickens.
Add dandelion to the mixture and heat gentle.
Season the mixture with sea salt and pepper to taste.

Basic Natural Nutrition as Mother Nature has provided

Sausage Dandelion Turnovers

1 lb. bulk pork sausage
⅓ cup chopped onion
3 cups chopped dandelion greens
1 ½ cups shredded sharp cheddar cheese
2 tsp. prepared mustard
1 tsp. dried marjoram
Sea salt and pepper to taste
1 loaf frozen bread dough, thawed
1 egg white beaten

In skillet, cook sausage and onion over medium heat until meat is no longer pink, drain. Stir in dandelion, cheese, mustard, marjoram, sea salt and pepper. Cook and stir until cheese is melted. Remove from heat, cool slightly.
Divide dough into 8 portions; roll each into a 6 inch circle.
Spoon ½ cup of meat mixture on half of each circle. Brush edges with egg white; fold dough over filling and press edges with a fork to seal. Place on greased baking sheets. Cover and let rise in a warm place for 20 mins.
Brush tops with egg whites; cut slits in top of each. Bake at 350°F for 20 mins or until golden brown.

Nutrition supplied as it's meant to be.
Our forefathers didn't have all the medicines of today. They got everything they needed from the land. Imagine, no fast food...

Side of Dandelion

1 tbsp. olive oil
½ cup chopped onion
2 garlic cloves, minced
3 tbsp. sour cream or low fat yogurt
2 tsp. honey prepared mustard
¼ tsp. ground nutmeg, sea salt and pepper
3 cups of dandelion greens, lightly packed

Heat olive oil in frying pan on medium. Add onion. Cook for 5 to 10 mins, stirring often, until softened.
Add garlic. Heat and stir for 2 mins until fragrant.
Combine next 5 ingredients in small cup. Add to onion mixture. Stir.
Add dandelion. Heat and stir until just wilted. Serve and enjoy.

Digest this - The earth keeps replenishing itself for us.

Dandelion Stuffed Tomatoes

8 tomatoes
Sea salt
2 cups fresh, blanched, chopped dandelion greens
¼ cup softened butter or olive oil
1 cup chopped onion
½ cup grated carrots, chopped celery, and green pepper
2 eggs
½ cup milk
1 cup seasoned dry bread crumbs
1 tsp. sea salt and pepper, parsley flakes
Grated parmesan or cheddar cheese or your choice

Cut tops of tomatoes. Scoop out pulp. Sprinkle tomato cup with sea salt. Turn up side down to drain.
Cook dandelion in small amount of water for 3 min. Drain well.
Put butter or olive oil, onion, carrot, celery and green pepper into frying pan. Sauté until onion is soft and clear.
Add dandelion and remove from heat.
Beat eggs until frothy. Add milk, bread crumbs, sea salt, pepper and parsley. Mix with dandelion mixture.
Stuff the tomatoes.
Sprinkle with cheese. Arrange in greased baking pan. Bake uncovered at 350°F for 20 - 25 mins.

Imagine no Heart Disease...
Imagine no Diabetes...

Dandelion Stuffing

3 cups blanched, chopped dandelion greens, thawed
½ cup butter or olive oil
¼ lb. mushrooms, thinly sliced
1 cup diced celery
½ cup chopped onion
3 cups fresh bread crumbs
15 oz. ricotta cheese
1 egg
1 tbsp. minced parsley
1 tsp. sea salt
½ tsp. poultry seasoning
½ tsp. pepper

Squeeze dandelion dry with paper towel.
In saucepan over medium heat, in hot butter or olive oil; cook mushrooms, celery and onion until tender, about 5 minutes, stirring occasionally. Remove from heat.
Add remaining ingredients and dandelion; mix well in a casserole dish with no lid. Bake at 350 degrees for approximately ½ hour or until top is golden brown.

Imagine; no worldwide Hunger...

Creamy Baked Dandelion Greens

2 tbsp. butter or olive oil
1 small onion, finely chopped
2 tbsp. flour
1 tsp. sea salt and pepper
1 cup milk
2 eggs, separated
5 cups dandelion greens, finely chopped, boiled. Cook 5 min. in small amount of water and then drain well.

Grease baking dish. In saucepan over medium heat, in hot butter or olive oil, cook onion until tender, about 5 minutes. Stir in flour, sea salt and pepper until blended. Gradually stir in milk; cook, stirring, until sauce boils and is slightly thickened.
Preheat oven to 350°F. In small bowl with fork, beat egg yolks slightly. Into yolks, stir small amount of hot sauce; slowly pour yolk mixture into sauce, stirring rapidly to prevent lumping. Cook stirring constantly, until thickened.
Remove from heat; stir in dandelion greens.
In small bowl, with mixer at high speed, beat egg whites until stiff peaks form. With wire whisk, gently fold egg whites into dandelion mixture. Pour into baking dish. Bake 20 - 25 mins. Enjoy.

Imagine; No Cancer...

Sautéed Dandelion with Spices

In saucepan;
Heat 1 tsp. olive oil over medium heat
Fry 1 onion, chopped, until softened

Add;
1 ½ tsp. mild curry paste or powder
2 cloves of garlic, minced
¼ tsp. sea salt
1 pinch of ground cloves

Add;
3 cups fresh dandelion greens. Cook, drained and chopped, stirring in above mixture until blended.

Imagine; no Arthritis...

Acorn Squash Filled with Savory Dandelion

4 small acorn squash
2 tbsp. olive oil
3 cups cooked dandelion greens, drained
8 oz. ricotta cheese
1 tbsp. grated parmesan cheese
¼ tsp. pepper
⅛ tsp. sea salt and a touch of ground nutmeg

Preheat oven to 325°F. Cut squash crosswise in half. Scoop out seeds and fibers; discard. Brush insides and outsides of squash halves with olive oil.
Place in large shallow roasting pan. Bake, uncovered, 35-40 mins or until tender when pierced with fork.
In medium bowl, combine dandelion greens, ricotta cheese, parmesan cheese, pepper, sea salt and nutmeg.
Spoon equal amounts of dandelion mixture into squash halves. Bake uncovered, an additional 10-15 minutes. Enjoy.

Imagine; no Gout...

Deborah Richmond

Emerald Green Dandelion Rice

3 cups cooked rice
3 cups chopped dandelion greens
1 cup shredded cheddar cheese
1 cup half-and-half cream
½ cup chopped onion
1 tsp. sea salt

In bowl, combine all ingredients. Transfer to a greased baking dish. Cover and bake at 350°F for 25-35 mins or until heated through.

Imagine; no Kidney or Liver Disease...

Dandelions with Mushrooms

8 cups dandelion greens, well washed and trimmed
Sea salt and pepper to taste
Butter or olive oil
1 tbsp. chopped onion
1 lb. mushrooms, sliced
3½ tbsp. flour
1¼ cups milk

Cook dandelion, covered, in a small quantity, less than 1 cup, of boiling sea salted water until tender, approximately 3 to 5 minutes.
Drain well, reserving liquid. Chop dandelion coarsely. Boil down reserved liquid to one-half cup.
Preheat oven to 350°F.
Season dandelion with sea salt, pepper, melted butter or olive oil. Pack in buttered custard cup and place in a pan of hot water.
Cover with baking sheet and bake until thoroughly heated, about 15 minutes.
Meanwhile add one half tsp. sea salt to onion and mushrooms and cook in 2 tbsp. butter or olive oil until lightly browned, stirring constantly. Add flour and mix well. Add milk gradually and cook, stirring constantly, until thickened.
Add dandelion liquid, correct seasonings and reheat. Turn dandelion out of the molds and serve with sauce.

Imagine no depression...

Pan Sautéed Dandelion

4 – 6 cups shredded dandelion, cut crosswise into ½ in. lengths.

Place dandelion in a heavy saucepan.

Dribble over it, 2-3 tbsp. olive oil.

Add a very small amount of water (scarcely more than enough to cover bottom of pan.)

Cover and cook quickly over high heat.

Remove cover to stir through a couple of times.

Sprinkle with sea salt, pepper, and/or seasonings to taste, suggest garlic powder or a squeeze of lemon or a pinch of nutmeg

Total cooking time will be 5 to 7 minutes or when dandelion has wilted, is still green and has body.

Remove from heat and serve immediately.

This is my gift to you for your good Health!!!

Dandelion Main Course Meals

Dandelion and Chicken

4 boneless, skinless chicken breasts, halved
1 large egg, beaten
2 tbsp. olive oil
1 tsp. olive oil
½ chopped red pepper
2 tbsp. chopped onion
3 cups dandelion greens
1 tsp. sea salt
½ cup sour cream or low fat yogurt

Roll each chicken piece into egg until coated.
Heat 2 tbsp. olive oil in frying pan on medium. Add chicken. Cook for about 2 min per side until lightly browned. Transfer to greased baking dish. Cook uncovered, in 350°F oven for about 20 minutes until chicken is no longer pink and juices run clear. Transfer to serving dish. Keep warm.
Heat 1 tsp. olive oil in same frying pan on medium. Add red pepper and onion. Cook for 5 to 10 minutes stirring often, until onion is softened.
Add dandelion and sea salt. Heat and stir for about 3 minutes until heated through.
Add sour cream or low fat yogurt. Stir. Divide and spoon dandelion mixture onto 4 individual plates. Cut each chicken breast half into about 5 slices. Place 1 sliced chicken breast half on top of dandelion.

Living Dande Naturally.

Lamb with Dandelion Greens

1 tbsp. olive oil
2 lbs. lamb stew meat
2 cups sliced fresh white mushrooms
1 cup chopped onion
1 cup chopped red pepper
14 oz. can of diced tomatoes in juice
1 cup prepared chicken broth
2 tsp. fresh thyme leaves
½ tsp. sugar
¼ tsp. pepper and sea salt to taste
1 tbsp. water
1 tbsp. cornstarch
2 cups Fresh dandelion greens

Heat olive oil in frying pan on medium high. Add lamb in 2 batches. Cook 8-10 mins per batch, stirring occasionally, until browned.
Transfer to slow cooker.
Add mushrooms, onion and red pepper to same frying pan.
Cook on med 5 – 10 mins, stirring often, until onion is softened. Add to lamb, stir.
Combine next 6 ingredients in med bowl. Pour over lamb.
Stir well. Cover. Cook on high for 4 to 5 hrs. or low for 8 to 10 hrs.
Stir water into cornstarch in small cup until smooth. Add to lamb. Stir well. Cover. Cook on high for 5 to 10 mins until sauce is thickened.
Add dandelion greens, watch them wilt. Serve. Enjoy.

Dandelions offer health and vitality.

Dandelion Turkey Breast

1 turkey breast half, bone removed
5 strips of bacon or use turkey bacon
¾ cup chopped onion
3 tbsp. all-purpose flour
¾ tsp. dried tarragon
½ tsp. sea salt
¼ tsp. pepper
1½ cups milk
3 cups chopped dandelion greens
1 can (4 ½ oz.) sliced mushrooms, drained
1 tbsp. olive oil
⅓ cup cubed cheddar or mozzarella cheese

Cut lengthwise slit in turkey to within ½ inch of opposite side. Cover with plastic wrap and flatten to ½ inch thickness. Remove plastic, set aside.
In skillet, cook 2 bacon strips until crisp drain, reserving 2 tbsp. drippings or use tbsp. olive oil. Crumble bacon; set aside. Sauté onion in the drippings until tender, stir in flour, tarragon, sea salt and pepper until blended. Gradually stir in milk and cubed cheese chunks. Bring to a boil; cook and stir for 2 minutes or until thickened. Remove from heat. Refrigerate ½ cup of sauce. Add the dandelion greens, mushrooms and crumbled bacon to remaining sauce; spread over turkey breast. Starting at the short end, roll and tuck in ends; tie with kitchen string. Place on rack in greased roasting pan. Brush with olive oil. Cover loosely with foil. Bake at 350°F for 1 hour. Remove foil. Cut remaining bacon in half. Place over turkey. Bake 25-35 minutes longer.
Heat reserved sauce, serve with turkey.
Enjoy.

Making sense of your health

Dandelion Patties

3 ½ to 4 cups of cut up dandelion greens
1 ½ cups, cooked white rice
3 tbsp. flour
3 egg whites
2 tbsp. grated parmesan cheese
Sea salt and pepper to taste

Mix all ingredients together into paste like consistency.
Shape into small patties about 2 inches in diameter.
Spray patties with cooking spray or use olive oil and place in lightly greased heated skillet.
Cook in frying pan on medium high for 7-10 minutes each side or until both sides are crispy.

Plant nutrients produce the right stuff, like calcium, magnesium, potassium, and B vitamins your body needs and uses anyway.

Dandelion Casserole

6 cups dandelion leaves, chopped
2 cups cottage cheese
1 cup butter cut in pieces
1 ½ cups cheddar cheese, cubed
3 eggs, beaten
¼ cup of your choice of flour
1 tsp. sea salt

Thoroughly combine all ingredients in bowl.
Pour into greased crock pot.
Cover and cook on high 1 hr., then turn to low for 4-5 hours.

God gave them to us; know that they'll move us. Gather, clean & trim them. Blanche in small amount of boiling water for 2 min, drain and pack into muffin tins and/or ice cube trays. Freeze then pop out, put into freezer bags for use during the winter months with your meals.

Green Tuna Melt

170 g can tuna
2 tbsp. low fat plain yogurt
1 tbsp. freshly squeezed lemon juice
Generous pinches of dried oregano leaves, sea salt, and ground black pepper
1 cup dandelion greens
½ red or yellow peppers
Several thin slices of red onion
¾ cup grated mozzarella or cheddar cheese
2 slices your favorite bread

Set oven rack about 6 in. from broiler element. Preheat broiler. Drain tuna and place in small bowl. Stir in low fat yogurt, lemon juice, oregano, sea salt and pepper. Coarsely chop dandelion. Thinly slice pepper and onion into long strips. Grate cheese. Place a wire rack on a rimmed baking sheet. Place bread on rack. Divide tuna between slices and spread to edges. Top with dandelion, pepper and onion. Sprinkle with cheese.
Broil until cheese melts 3-4 mins.
Enjoy!

Chinese folk healers and Dr's treat a host of cancers with dandelion - why shouldn't we?

Powerful Dandelion Medley

½ cup raspberry flavored vinaigrette dressing, divided
1 ½ cups thinly sliced carrots
2 cups broccoli florets
4 cups cut dandelion greens
½ cup grated mozzarella or marble cheese
2 to 3 tbsp. left over roast beef, chicken, or the least healthy choice bacon cut up fine.

Bring ¼ cup of dressing and carrots to boil in medium saucepan. Reduce heat to low; cover and simmer 4 minutes. Stir in broccoli, cover and continue to simmer until crisp and tender. Toss remaining ingredients with hot vegetables in saucepan. Serve on the side or over cooked rice.
Feel the Joy it brings.

Deborah Richmond

Tuna-Dandelion Casserole

Cook Time: 12 to 15 minutes
Makes: 4 servings

3 ½ to 4 cups dandelion
1 can of tuna fish
1 can of sliced mushrooms
2 tbsp. lemon juice
2 tbsp. butter or olive oil
1 tbsp. minced onion
2 tbsp. all-purpose flour
¼ tsp. sea salt
⅛ tsp. pepper
1 egg, lightly beaten
½ cup crumbled potato chips

Rinse dandelion in cold water; drain well. Cut in pieces. Place in 2-quart micro proof casserole. Cook, covered, on high (max power) 1 to 2 minutes or until dandelion is limp. Drain well, set aside. Drain tuna, set aside. Drain mushrooms, pouring liquid into 1 cup measure. Set mushrooms aside. Add lemon juice and enough water to make 1 cup liquid. Place 2 tablespoons butter or olive oil in 4-cup glass measure. Cook on high, (max power) 45 seconds, or until melted. Add onion, flour, sea salt, and pepper, stirring well. Briskly stir in mushroom-lemon liquid. Cook uncovered, on medium power for 5 minutes, or until thick, stirring twice during cooking time. Add a small amount of sauce to egg, beat well, and return all too hot sauce. Stir mushrooms into sauce. Place well-drained dandelion in 2 ½ quart micro proof casserole dish. Flake tuna in small chunks over dandelion. Pour sauce over top. Sprinkle with crumbled potato chips. Cook, uncovered, on high, (max power) 4 minutes. Let stand 2 to 3 minutes before serving.

Dandelions are good for night blindness as stated in a 1952 medical journal

Dandelion Chicken Stuffed Red Peppers

Serves: 4

4 large red bell peppers
4 cups chopped fresh dandelion
10 oz. package fresh mushrooms, diced
2 cloves of garlic, minced
2 cups diced cooked chicken
1 cups prepared tomato-basil sauce
½ cup shredded parmesan cheese
Bunch of green onion, rinsed and chopped
Olive oil

Preheat oven to 400°F. Mist an 8-inch square baking dish with cooking spray. Cut tops off bell peppers (stem end) and remove seeds and ribbing; stand peppers right in prepared dish. Set aside.
In a skillet with olive oil, sauté dandelions, mushrooms, green onions and minced garlic. Cook over medium heat until softened, about 4 minutes. Add chicken to tomato-basil sauce; cook 3 to 4 minutes, until heated. Remove pan from heat.
Spoon ½ cup of dandelion chicken mixture into each pepper. Top with 1 tbsp. parmesan cheese. Fill peppers with and remaining mixture, evenly divided. Top with remaining cheese.
Cover peppers with foil and bake 55 to 60 minutes, or until peppers are tender. Serve with crusty bread.

Dandelions are full of vitamins & minerals. So by increasing your intake it makes your body work better.

Dandelion & Black Eyed Peas

1 lb. diced black-eyed peas
2 cups chopped onion
1 ½ tbsp fresh minced garlic (about 5 cloves)
1 cup chopped tomatoes
4 to 8 cups fresh dandelion
3 tbsp. fresh, minced parsley
2 tbsp. fresh, minced thyme
1 tbsp. olive oil
Add sea salt and black pepper to taste.

Rinse beans, and soak overnight (6-8 hours) in a large pot (8 cups of water) or quick soak them by bringing them to a rapid boil for 2 minutes. Remove from water afterwards. When you're ready to cook them, heat olive oil in a large pot over medium heat. Add onion and sauté until golden.
Add beans, garlic, sea salt, pepper and 6-8 cups of water. Cover, bring to a boil, lower heat to a simmer and cook for about 1 hour.
Add dandelion, tomatoes, thyme, and parsley and cook for 30 minutes or so until desired tenderness. Add water if needed.

*Dandelions grow freely.
I'm telling you, if you wanted to be an Entrepreneur, gardener, or farmer of dandelions, there are plenty of opportunity around.*

Dande Burgers

1 lb. ground hamburger
1 cup chopped fresh dandelion
½ cup dry bread crumbs
½ cup chopped onion
¼ cup low fat yogurt OR add one egg beaten
2 tbsp. Worcestershire sauce
1 clove garlic, minced
¼ tsp. pepper

Combine all ingredients in a large bowl. Mix thoroughly. Shape into 4 large patties. Place patties on oiled grill. Grill over medium-high heat 4-6 minutes on each side, until no longer pink in center. Serve with mozzarella cheese and red pepper slices, if desired.

The Universe took action towards supplying us with a sustainable, local green food that has Benefits.
Shouldn't we be using our Dandelions?

Cheesy Dandelion Burgers

1 pouch onion soup mix
1 ½ lbs. ground beef
3 ½ to 4 cups chopped dandelion
1 cup shredded mozzarella cheese

In large bowl, combine all ingredients. Shape into 8 patties. Barbeque or broil on medium high heat, 5-7 minutes per side.

Enjoy on a hot Summer day.

Treating my Body to what it needs isn't a freak of Nature. Our bodies immune boosting, biologically welcomes it, naturally responds well to it.

Dandelion Sandwich filling

1 ½ cups
shredded fresh dandelion
1 hard-cooked egg, chopped
1 tsp. onion juice
Sea salt and pepper
1 tbsp. low fat yogurt
Celery
Combine ingredients; mix lightly. Spread on buttered bread.

I love my dandelion – stay with your greens and gradually get healthier for it.
"Enjoy".

Dandelion and Apple Pizza with fresh Basil

1 small pre-made or frozen pizza shell
½ cup of apple sauce
1 ½ cups of scissor cut or finely chopped dandelions leaves
1 medium apple, peeled and thinly sliced
½ of one small onion, sliced or diced
½ cup shredded mozzarella cheese
1 tbsp. of chopped fresh basil

Place the pizza on a baking sheet and evenly distribute the apple sauce on top.
Add the dandelions, then the apples and onion and top with cheese and fresh basil.
Bake the pizza in a preheated oven at 325°F for about 15 min, or until the cheese is bubbling. Allow the pizza to cool until it is just warm.
Slice into 4 pieces and serve.

Hint: Try using sliced pear instead of apple. Replace the mozzarella with other types of cheese, such as cheddar, feta etc.

Let's have a Healthy Time of it, before there's no time left.

Baked Dandelion with Brown Rice & Cheese

4 cups fresh dandelion, washed and chopped
Brown rice measured to the 8 fl. oz. level in a measuring cup
16 fl. oz. hot water
1 onion, finely chopped
1 tbsp. olive oil
1 tsp. butter
4 oz. grated cheddar cheese
2 large eggs, beaten
2 tbsp. chopped parsley
2 tbsp. whole wheat breadcrumbs
1 tbsp. melted butter
Couple of pinches cayenne pepper or to taste
Nutmeg
Sea salt and pepper

Melt the butter and olive oil in a saucepan and soften the onion in it, then stir in the rice to get it nicely coated with oil. Add the hot water, stir once, and simmer gently with a lid on for 40 mins. or until the liquid has been absorbed and the grains are tender.
As soon as the rice is cooked, cool it in a bowl, and then combine it with the grated cheese. Stir in the eggs and parsley followed by the chopped dandelion. Season well and add a good grating of nutmeg.
Now place the mixture into a large oiled pie dish, mix the breadcrumbs with the melted butter and cayenne and sprinkle over top. Bake for 35 mins. at 350°F.

Take time for yourself!

Dande-Mashed Potato Casserole

Bake 400°F for 20 mins.
Cook and mash 4 large potatoes

Add:
⅓ cup sour cream or low fat yogurt – plain
1 tsp. sea salt
Dash pepper
¼ cup butter or olive oil
Add just enough milk to bring to proper consistency and beat until fluffy. Add:
⅛ tsp. dill seed
2 tbsp. chives chopped
2 cups cooked dandelion, well drained and chopped.
Mix everything well, and place in greased casserole dish and top with ½ cup grated cheddar cheese.
This can be made a day or two ahead and refrigerated. Will freeze if needed

Take care of you first

Dandelion Casserole

Preheat oven to 350°F
Grease a 9-inch square casserole.
Cook until just tender in a very small amount of water, 3 ½ to 4 cups of dandelion

In prepared casserole, arrange 4 slices of bread without crusts
Top with 1 package processed cheddar cheese slices
Spread drained dandelion over top and sprinkle with
1 ½ cups cubed cooked ham
Arrange on top, overlapping slightly 6 bread slices, halved
Beat together and pour over top
 1 ½ cups milk
½ tsp. dry mustard
3 eggs
¼ tsp. sea salt
Dot with 1 tbsp. butter or olive oil
Bake in preheated 350°F oven for 45 to 50 minutes or until egg mixture is just set. Serve hot.

Dandelions assist in waste - waist management.

Dandelion and Egg Casserole

¼ cup butter or olive oil
¼ cup flour
½ tsp. sea salt
¼ tsp. paprika
2 cups milk
1 cup bread crumbs
2 cups chopped, cooked dandelion
4 eggs, hard boiled, peeled and sliced
4 slices Cheddar Cheese

-Melt butter or olive oil, stir in flour, sea salt, paprika and milk and cook, stirring constantly, until thickened.

-In greased baking dish, assemble casserole as follows: half the bread crumbs, half the dandelion, half the eggs, one-third of the sauce, half the cheese, rest of dandelion, rest of eggs, one-third of the sauce, rest of cheese, rest of sauce and rest of bread crumbs. Bake at 325°F for 35-40 minutes. Serves 4

Many of the plants that we consider garden weeds were eaten by the first European settlers in America. In fact many of these weeds were introduced here as a valuable source of food.

Dandelion with Two Cheeses

8 cups dandelion
5 tbsp. olive oil or butter
1 cup ricotta cheese or small-curd light cottage cheese
1 egg
3 tbsp. flour
¼ tsp. sea salt
Dash or pepper and nutmeg
3 tbsp. parmesan cheese

Cook dandelion. Drain dandelion a sieve colander, pressing out most of the liquid with back of large spoon. Chop dandelion fine. Melt 3 tbsp. of olive oil or butter in same pot. Remove from heat. Add chopped dandelion, ricotta cheese, egg, flour, sea salt, pepper and nutmeg. Beat with a spoon until thoroughly mixed.
Place the mixture in a buttered baking dish. Dot with remaining butter or olive oil and sprinkle with parmesan cheese. Bake, uncovered for 10 minutes or until the cheese melts

Reap what is sown from the Dandelion seed, and reap its benefits

Dandelion Cream Cheese Pie

Although this pie has no crust, the wheat germ bakes to a crispy texture. Resulting in a quiche like dish.

3 cups dandelion
8 oz. cream cheese
1 tbsp. minced onion
Dash nutmeg
6 eggs
Wheat germ
¼ lb. Cheddar cheese, sliced
Paprika
1 tbsp. flour
1 tsp. water

-Cook dandelion, drain and press out excess water. Soften cream cheese and add dandelion, onion and nutmeg. Beat 5 of the eggs and stir into the dandelion mixture.
-Grease sides and bottom of a pie plate, sprinkle it with wheat germ and pour in dandelion mixture. Cover with sliced cheese and sprinkle with paprika.
-Beat remaining egg with flour and water and pour over the cheese. Bake at 350°F for 35 to 45 minutes, until top is lightly browned.

My friend Joyce said – sometimes you just have to take what Nature gives you.

Dandelion Pie

¼ cup olive oil
1 ¼ cups fine (your choice bread) crumbs
2 tbsp. parmesan cheese
3 cups of dandelion, chopped
2 green onions thinly sliced
2 cups 2% creamed cottage cheese
¼ cup crumbled feta cheese
2 tbsp. spelt, millet, or rice flour
2 eggs, beaten
1 tbsp. chopped fresh dill weed
¼ tsp. sea salt and pepper

Preheat oven to 350°F. In bowl, mix olive oil, bread crumbs and Parmesan cheese. Pat ¾ of this mixture into pie plate.
In another bowl, mix dandelion, cottage cheese, feta, flour.
Add eggs, dill weed, sea salt and pepper. Pour mixture into pie shell. Sprinkle remaining crumbs on top.
Bake for 40 minutes or until center looks and feels set. Serve hot or cold.

Knowledge is power

Shepherds Green Pie

1 lb. of lean ground beef
1 recipe of Brown Sauce (see recipe below)
Left over mashed potatoes
Top with 2 oz. crumbled cheese

- Start to brown meat, combine with sauce
- Turn into casserole dish
- Cover with mashed potatoes
- Sprinkle with cheese
- Re-heat and brown towards top of hot oven (425°F) for 15 to 20 min.

Brown Sauce
1 oz. of butter
1 teaspoon olive oil
1 oz. chopped ham or bacon
½ small, peeled onion
2 cups fresh cut dandelion or add ¾ to 1 cup of dandelion soup (refer to soup section)
1 oz. mushrooms and stalks
½ small, peeled carrot
1 oz. of flour
½ pint beef stock or OXO cube
1 level dessert spoon tomato puree (or 1 small chopped tomato)
1 small bay leaf
2 sprigs parsley

Put butter and olive oil into pan. Heat both till sizzling. Add ham or bacon, chopped onion, celery, mushrooms with stalks and sliced carrots. Sauté 7-10 min until golden. Add flour and cook stirring until it becomes light brown. Add dandelion soup or your 2 cups fresh cut leaves and stalk. Gradually blend in beef stock let boil and thicken. Add tomato and bay leaf and parsley. Cover pan let simmer 10 min. Season with sea salt and pepper, add browned ground beef.
Put in casserole dish, top with mashed potatoes and grated cheese. Reheat to 425°F. Bake for 15 to 20 mins.

Grow up green.

Dande Quesadilla

2 cups 1% cottage cheese
2 cloves of garlic, minced
2 tbsp. grated Parmesan cheese
¼ tsp. pepper
3 ½ to 4 cups dandelion
12 - 10 inch tortilla shells
1 can of refried beans
1 ¼ cups of salsa
½ cup shredded mozzarella cheese

In food processor or bowl, blend cottage cheese, garlic, parmesan cheese and pepper until smooth. Stir dandelion into cheese mixture. Place one tortilla shell on pizza sheet. Spread about ⅔ cup refried beans over tortilla. Cover with another tortilla shell. Spread ½ cup of salsa on top; cover with another tortilla shell; spread 1 cup of cheese and dandelion mixture on top. Add another tortilla shell. Starting with refried beans, repeat layers two or more times.
Arrange sliced tomatoes and mozzarella cheese on top.
Bake at 350°F for 45-60 mins. Cut into wedges and serve.

Feel "Dande" when you eat Dandelions

Turkey and Dandelion Ranch Wraps

2 cups chopped cooked turkey
2 cups cut up dandelion greens
½ cup chopped red bell pepper
½ cup frozen kernel corn, thawed
¼ cup thinly sliced green onion
¼ cup light ranch salad dressing
6 flour tortillas

In bowl, combine turkey, dandelion, red pepper, corn, onion and dressing Spoon turkey mixture evenly down the center of each tortilla. Fold bottom of edge of each tortilla 1 inch over turkey mixture. Fold sides of tortilla to center, overlapping edges. Serve immediately or wrap individually and refrigerate for up to four hours.

People have to start thinking differently about health. Did your mother ever tell you to eat your Greens? If not, I am.

Hazelnut Chicken rolls with Dandelion

6 boneless skinless chicken breasts
3 ½ to 4 cups chopped dandelion, cooked and pressed dry
2 tbsp. grated parmesan cheese
1 egg, beaten
½ cup hazelnuts, finely chopped
¼ cup whole wheat flour or spelt flour
¼ tsp. pepper
1 tbsp. butter
2 tbsp. olive oil
¼ cup dry white wine

Pound your chicken thin. Spoon some dandelion and 1 tsp. Parmesan cheese in each chicken breast.
Roll from narrow end. Fasten with toothpick.
In shallow dish, combine hazelnuts, flour and pepper.
Dip rolls into beaten egg and then roll in nut mixture.
In baking dish, heat butter and olive oil.
Place rolls in pan and bake at 375°F for 45 mins.
Remove rolls to heated platter. Remove toothpicks.
Add wine to pan and stir to loosen any brown bits.
Pour over chicken.

Whose income are you supplementing with whose nutrients?

Warm Gingered Chicken with Dande Greens

½ cup low fat yogurt
2 tsp. red wine vinegar
1 tsp. soy sauce
1 tsp. honey
¼ tsp. ground ginger
Pinch of sea salt
1 tbsp. orange juice
4 boneless, skinless chicken breasts
6 cups mixed baby dandegreen
2 oranges, peeled and sectioned

In a small bowl, blend low fat yogurt, vinegar, soy sauce, honey, ginger and sea salt. Set aside ¼ cup of the low fat yogurt mixture for grilling. Stir orange juice into remaining low fat yogurt mixture and reserve for tossing with the dandegreen.
Grill or broil chicken, brushing with reserved ¼ cup low fat yogurt mixture, 12 minutes or until chicken is cooked turning once. In large bowl, toss dande greens with reserved orange juice mixture. To serve, arrange sliced chicken over greens. Top with orange slices.

Face health issues head on. Your head is clear on Dandelions

Chicken and Dandelion Rice

1 tbsp. olive oil
1 lb. boneless, skinless chicken breasts cut into bite size pieces
4 cups dandelion, washed and dried
1 ½ cups of quick cook rice, uncooked
1 cup cherry or grape tomatoes
10 oz. chicken broth
½ cup water
¼ cup grated Parmesan cheese

Heat olive oil in large, deep, nonstick skillet on medium high heat. Add chicken; cook and stir 10 min or until chicken is cooked through.
Add dandelion, rice, tomatoes, broth and water.
Mix well.
Bring to a boil. Reduce heat to low and cover. Simmer 5 min stirring occasionally. Sprinkle parmesan cheese over top and serve.

Dandelions
What part of the plant do you use? All of the dark greens are used like spinach. Use roots for tea and medicine to clean up your internal environment.

Rice size Pasta with Chicken, Dandelion and Walnuts

1 cup chopped walnuts
1 lb. boneless skinless chicken breasts
½ tsp. each sea salt and pepper
2 tbsp. extra-virgin olive oil
4 cloves garlic, minced
3 ½ to 4 cups fresh dandelion
½ cup chicken stock
2 tbsp. wine vinegar
5 cups small pasta or penne pasta
½ cup grated parmesan cheese

In large nonstick skillet, toast walnuts over medium heat, shaking pan occasionally, until fragrant, about 5 minutes. Remove from pan and set aside.
Slice chicken thinly across the grain; sprinkle with half each of the sea salt and pepper. In same skillet, heat oil over medium-high heat; sauté chicken, in two batches, until golden and no longer pink inside, about five minutes. Using slotted spoon, transfer chicken to bowl.
Add garlic, dandelion and remaining sea salt and pepper to pan; cover and cook over medium heat until dandelion begins to wilt, about 1 minute. Return chicken and any accumulated juices to pan. Stir in chicken stock and wine vinegar; bring to a simmer.
Meanwhile, in a large pot of boiling sea salted water, cook pasta until tender but firm, 8 to 10 minutes. Drain and return to pot. Add chicken mixture and walnuts; toss to coat. Serve sprinkled with parmesan cheese.

Makes four to six servings

Dandelions are just Dande

Cedar Baked Salmon with Dandelion

Cedar shingles and shims are available in lumber yards and in some grocery stores. They impart a special flavor to salmon when baking. You will need to soak 2 untreated cedar shingles or 1 pkg. of cedar shims in water at least 2 hrs, preferably overnight.

1 ½ lb. Atlantic salmon fillets
Grated rind and juice of 1 lime
1 ½ cups diagonally sliced asparagus
¼ cup julienne leeks
4 thin slices of red onion
¼ cup diagonally sliced celery
½ cup thickly sliced shitake mushrooms
2 medium tomatoes, seeded and cut into strips
8 fresh basil leaves, slivered
3 ½ to 4 cups dandelion
Sea salt and pepper

Place shims or shingles on baking sheet, lightly brushed with oil.
Remove skin and any bones from salmon, cut into serving size pieces and place on cedar. Sprinkle with lime rind and juice. Bake at 425°F for 10 to 15 mins or until fish flakes.
Meanwhile, in a steamer basket, combine asparagus, leek, onion and celery until partially cooked. Add mushrooms, tomatoes, basil, and dandelion and steam, just until tender crisp and dandelion is wilted.
Season with sea salt and pepper and serve with the cedar planked salmon.

Dandelions come from Mother Earth, pharmacist's can't duplicate Nature

Baked Salmon with Tomatoes, Dandelion & Mushrooms

4 salmon fillets
2 cups chopped dandelion
1 cup sliced mushrooms
1 medium tomato, chopped
⅓ cup Sundried Tomato and Oregano Dressing
Olive oil

Place salmon, skin sides down, in baking dish coated with olive oil. Mix remaining ingredients until well blended; spoon over salmon. Bake at 375°F for 20-25 mins or until salmon flakes easily when tested with fork.

Even the Dr. and his wife my grandmother worked for in the 1920's went to town near Ottawa every week and came home with Dandelions to eat for her family, from the market. This story should tell us something about our trips to the market or grocery.

Salmon with Dandelion

2 cups cooked or canned salmon
Milk
¼ cup butter (⅛ cup butter, ⅛ cup olive oil)
¼ cup flour
½ tsp. dry mustard
¼ tsp. sea salt
¼ tsp. Tabasco sauce
1 ½ cups grated cheese
2 cups cooked dandelion, drained

Preheat oven to 425°F.
Drain and flake salmon. Add enough milk to the salmon liquid to make 1 ½ cups.
In saucepan melt butter, add flour and stir with a wire whisk until blended. Meanwhile, bring milk mixture to a boil and add all at once to the butter-flour mixture, stirring vigorously with whisk until sauce is thickened and smooth.
Season the sauce with dry mustard, sea salt, and Tabasco and mix in one cup of cheese.
Place dandelions in floured individual greased casseroles, top with salmon and sauce and sprinkle with remaining cheese.
Bake uncovered for 15 mins.

Sometimes, it's bitter when you taste it, but it's good for you once you have taken it.

Country Vegetable Casserole

Prep: 25 mins
Bake 1 hour
Makes 8 to 10 servings

Topping
4 slices white bread
½ cup grated Parmesan or Asigao cheese
¼ cup butter or olive oil
⅛ cup of chives
Generous pinches of sea salt and pepper.

Filling
2 leeks
1 tbsp. butter
2 garlic cloves, minced
1 head cauliflower
1 each green and yellow pepper
1 zucchini
2 cups chopped Dandelion
½ cup all-purpose flour
1 tsp. dried sage leaves, crumbled
½ tsp. each sea salt and pepper
¼ tsp. ground nutmeg
3 tbsp. Dijon
1 ½ cups whipping cream

1. Preheat oven to 100°F. For topping, trim crust from bread. Place slices on a baking sheet. Toast in center of preheated oven until lightly golden, 3 to 4 min. per side. Tear toasted bread into large pieces and place in a food processor. Add ½ cup cheese, chives, butter or olive oil. Add sea salt and pepper. Pulse until coarse crumbs form.
2. Increase oven temperature to 375°F. Slice off and discard dark green tops. Cut roots of leeks in half lengthwise. Fan out and rinse under water to remove and grit. Thinly slice. Heat butter or
olive oil in a large frying pan over medium heat, add leeks and garlic.

(Continued on next page)

Stir often until leeks begin to soften, 3 to 5 min. Set aside in a large bowl.

3. Meanwhile, cut cauliflower into small bite sized pieces, and peppers into smaller bite-sized pieces. Slice zucchini in half lengthwise, and then slice crossways. Add to leeks. Squeeze excess water from cleaned dandelion. Add dandelion to vegetables. Sprinkle with ½ cup Parmesan, flour, sage, ½ tsp. (2 ml) each sea salt and pepper, nutmeg. Toss to evenly mix.

4. Turn into a lightly olive oiled 9 x 13 baking dish and evenly spread out. Gently press down to lightly pack. Using a fork beat Dijon into cream until evenly blended. Evenly pour over vegetables. Sprinkle bread crumbs over top. Cover pan tightly with foil.

5. Bake in center of pre-heated oven, 35 to 40 mins. Uncover and continue to bake until vegetables are fork-tender and topping is golden, about 15 to 20 more min. Let stand 10 to 15 min. before serving.

It could be a life changing day, for your life; try some dandelions.

Beef and Greens Stir-Fry

Prep: 10 minutes
Cooking time: 6 to 8 minutes
Makes: 4 servings

1 cup milk
2 tbsp. cornstarch
½ cup thick teriyaki sauce
1 tsp. packed brown sugar
1 tsp. sesame oil (optional)
1 tbsp. olive oil
1 lb. stir-fry beef strips
1 tbsp. sesame seeds
2 cloves of garlic, minced
¼ tsp. sea salt
1 tbsp. rice vinegar or white wine vinegar
4 cups chopped dandelion, and 4 cups leafy greens (bokchoy, Swiss chard and/or spinach) or frozen mixed Oriental-style vegetables thawed.

1. In a bowl, whisk a little of the milk into cornstarch to make a smooth paste. Whisk in remaining Milk, teriyaki sauce, brown sugar and sesame oil (if using); set aside.
2. In a wok or non-stick skillet, heat olive oil over high heat; stir-fry beef, sesame seeds, garlic and sea salt for 5 min or until beef is browned. Whisk milk mixture and pour into wok. Cook about 3 min stirring often or until sauce is thickened. Stir in greens; cook, stirring, just until greens are wilted and hot, about 1 min. Stir in vinegar. Garnish with additional sesame seeds, if desired. Enjoy!

Earthly delights

Dandelion Meat Wraps

Whole-wheat tortilla

1) Fill with chicken or turkey breast, ham or lean roast beef and dandelions, tomatoes, peppers or other veggies; flavor with 1 tbsp. Parmesan or feta cheese, Italian dressing and/or oil and vinegar.

2) Fill with skinless chicken breast, lean beef, lean pork or shrimp; black beans; brown rice; salsa; dandelions and/or lettuce; and/or fresh guacamole; Italian dressing and/or oil and vinegar .

Life is a journey, don't you think it's also a learning process.

Dandelion Stuffed Chicken

1 cup dandelion
¼ finely chopped onion
1 clove of garlic, crushed or grated
⅓ tsp. red-pepper flakes
2 tsp. olive oil
¼ grated Parmesan cheese
2 tbsp. chopped dry-packed sun-dried tomatoes
4 chicken cutlets (about 4 oz. each) or 4 chicken breast halves trimmed and pounded thin into cutlets.
½ cup chicken broth or dry white wine.

1. Prepare Dandelion by immersing them into 3 cups of boiling water for 2 minutes. Transfer to strainer and dip into ice water. Immediately remove them and press firmly into strainer with back of slotted spoon or squeeze to remove excess moisture. There should be ½ cup dandelions.
2. Meanwhile, combine onion, garlic, red pepper flakes, 1 tsp. of the olive oil, and 1 tbsp. water in a medium non-stick skillet. Turn heat to medium; when onion starts to sizzle, turn heat to low, cover, and cook, stirring, until softened, about 3 minutes. In small bowl, stir together onion mixture, cheese, and dandelions. Set aside for step 5.
3. Sprinkle tomatoes evenly on smooth side of chicken.
4. Divide dandelion mixture among cutlets. Spread to edges of 3 sides, leaving about 1 inch at narrow tip free of Dandelion. Loosely roll chicken, ending with narrow tip, and secure with wooden picks.
5. Add remaining 1 tsp. olive oil to skillet. Add chicken and cook over medium heat, turning, until golden brown on all sides, about 10 min. Add broth, cover, and cook over low heat, about 7 min. Uncover and transfer rolls to serving platter. Cover with foil to keep warm.
6. Boil juices in skillet until reduced to a glaze, about 5 minutes. Diagonally slice rolls into inch-thick pieces, drizzle with pan juices, and serve.

Dogs eat greens when sick so they will fell better

Bay Scallops with Linguine, Dill and Mushrooms

¾ cup cooked pasta
½ lb. scallops, cleaned & thinly sliced
1 tbsp. butter or olive oil
1 tsp. minced garlic
½ tsp. dried dill
1 tbsp. minced red onion
1 cup sliced mushrooms
1 cup dandelion greens, washed & cut into bite size pieces
Sea salt and pepper to taste

Sauté scallops in butter or olive oil with garlic, dill, red onion, mushrooms, sea salt and pepper until cooked, about 5 mins over medium heat.
Toss in the cooked pasta and dandelion greens heat until dandelion greens are wilted.
Top with fresh grated parmesan cheese and place on the plate in a thin line with warm diced tomatoes around the edge of the plate.

Dandelions, better known as "Piss-a-beds" in many parts of Canada.

Dandelion Stuffed Cod

½ cup nuts, any type you like
2 cups dandelion greens, cleaned and cut up small
1 tbsp. onion, celery and garlic, minced
1 tsp. chili powder
½ tsp. dill, dried
1 cup ricotta or cottage cheese
1 cup green tomato, diced
2 lbs. cod fish fillets
Sea salt and pepper to taste

Place all ingredients, except for tomatoes and fish, into a blender and blend well. Pour mixture into a bowl and add in the diced tomatoes and mix by hand, until tomatoes are evenly mixed in. Set aside.
Clean fish and lay flat. Use approx. 1-3 tbsp. of filling over fillet, and roll it like a log.
Place in shallow baking dish with a 1 inch space between each fillet. Bake for 20 mins at 350°F.

Toilet paper was earlier described as the newfangled roll, as soft as Dandelion fluff. Someone probably thought of that while on their way to an outside outhouse.

Pizza on Pita

Use whole wheat or plain pita bread; butter both sides with garlic butter. Then add a layer of pizza sauce.
Then layer ingredients of choice:

Onion
Green pepper
Tomatoes
Cooked sausage
Cooked hamburger
Mushrooms
Dandelion greens
Ham
Anchovies
Salami
Pepperoni
Bacon
Pineapple

Cover with cheese. Cook at 350°F for 20 mins.

Dandelions are good for the Biology & physiology of our bodies, & our sexual desire.

Chicken Breasts with Dandelion Salad

Makes 4 servings

4 boneless chicken breasts
4 cups cut up dandelions
2 cups cubed English cucumber
1 cup chopped tomatoes
⅓ cup crumbled feta cheese
¼ cup pitted black olives, halved

Dressing:

¼ cup red wine
¼ cup extra-virgin olive oil
2 tbsp. lemon juice
2 tsp. granulated sugar
3 cloves of garlic, minced
½ tsp. each dried oregano and mint
¼ tsp. each sea salt and pepper

1. Place chicken in small roasting pan; set aside.

Dressing: In measuring cup, whisk together vinegar, olive oil, lemon juice, sugar, garlic, oregano, mint, sea salt and pepper; pour ⅓ cup over chicken, roast in 400°F oven, turning once, until no longer pink inside, about 10 minutes. Broil until golden, about 2 minutes.

2. Meanwhile, in large bowl, toss together dandelion, cucumber, tomatoes, feta cheese, olives and remaining dressing until coated. Divide salad among plates.

3. Thinly slice chicken; arrange over salad.

Simply delicious
temping new recipes that are green!

Garlic Dandelion Sandwich

2 slices whole grain bread or choice of bread
½ cucumber; peeled and sliced thinly
1 small tomato sliced thinly
1 - 2 garlic cloves
½ cup Dandelion leaves
Low fat yogurt to taste

Spread each slice of bread (fresh or toasted) with low fat plain yogurt. Slice or mince the garlic clove and add to the bread. Lay cut up dandelions on one slice of the bread and then pile on the thinly sliced cucumber and tomato. Add sea salt and pepper to taste if wanted. Top with the other slice of bread and enjoy!

A practical Nurse with practical idea's

Dandelion Oriental

Prep: 4-5 minutes
Makes: 4 Servings

2 cups dandelion, washed and cut up
1 can sliced water chestnuts, drained
1 or 2 green onions, sliced
2 tbsp. olive oil
2 tbsp. wine vinegar
2 tbsp. soy sauce
1 tsp. sugar

In 2-quart micro proof casserole, place dandelion, water chestnuts, and onions. Cook covered, on High 3 to 4 minutes, or until dandelion is limp. Stir, set aside covered. In 1 cup glass; place olive oil, wine vinegar, soy sauce, and sugar. Cook on High for 1 minute. Pour over Dandelion, toss, and serve hot.

I have a unique progressive social perspective and a strong sense of values.

Dandelion Chicken Stuffed Red Peppers

Serves: 4

4 large red bell peppers
4 cups chopped fresh dandelion
10 oz. package fresh mushrooms, diced
2 cloves of garlic, minced
2 cups diced cooked chicken
1 cup prepared tomato-basil sauce
½ cup shredded parmesan cheese
Bunch of green onion, rinsed and chopped

1. Preheat oven to 400°F. Coat 8 inch square baking dish with olive oil. Cut tops off bell peppers (stem end) and remove seeds and ribbing; stand peppers right in prepared dish. Set aside.
2. In a skillet, add olive oil, sauté dandelions, mushrooms, green onions and garlic over medium heat until softened, about 4 minutes. Add chicken and tomato-basil sauce; cook 3 to 4 minutes, until heated through. Remove from heat.
3. Spoon ½ cup of dandelion chicken mixture into each pepper. Top with 1 tbsp. Parmesan cheese. Fill peppers with and remaining mixture, divided evenly, and top with remaining cheese.
4. Cover peppers with foil and bake 55 to 60 minutes, or until peppers are tender. Serve with crusty bread.

The information in this book could benefit you in the care of your health and wellness.

Grilled Chicken over Dandelion

1 to 2 tbsp. olive oil
1 tbsp. cider vinegar
1 garlic clove, minced
1 tsp. dried oregano
Cayenne pepper to taste
¼ tsp. sea salt
Dash of pepper
4 boneless, skinless chicken breast halves
Sautéed Dandelion:
1 green onion, finely chopped
1 - 2 garlic cloves, minced
1 - 2 tbsp. olive oil
½ lb. fresh mushrooms, sliced
2 cups fresh dandelion greens cut up

In bowl combine the first 8 ingredients; mix well, spoon over chicken. Grill or pan fry uncovered over medium heat for 7-10 min on each side.
In large skillet sauté, onion and garlic in oil for approx 1 min. Stir in mushrooms; sauté until tender. Add dandelion. Sauté until wilted. Transfer to serving plate; top with chicken.

A Dandelion Seed Fund to help others, because collecting seed is not really a new concept! It only makes sense, birds do it, so do mothers, fathers, and grandmas. For generations people have scrounged, hunted, picked from their environment. Food is for survival for themselves, and their family.

Dandelion Teasers

Collecting and Preserving

After collecting fresh dandelion plants you may want to use some of the greens fresh, dried or freeze the rest for winter. For freezing, blanch dandelions by bringing lots of unsalted water to a rolling boil in a large open stockpot. Dip the greens in the boiling water for 30 to 40 seconds. Immediately remove with a slotted spoon or strainer to a large colander filled with ice water. After the greens are chilled, drain and pack them whole in muffin tins or chopped in ice cube trays. Once frozen, pop them out and store in freezer bags in the freezer for later use in your recipes. My friend, Donelda says she fills ice cube trays with water and finely cut up dandelion to freeze to put in drinks or to add to smoothies. She also chops and dries the leaves to put into a shaker bottle to add to recipes, similar to dried parsley flakes.

Following George Carins' suggestions you may want to warm dry the roots and try his approach to help "cure" cancer and/or other ailments or use them for losing weight.

Dandelion and Cheese Pancakes

⅔ cup chopped dandelion greens
3 eggs
1 cup milk
½ cup flour
⅓ cup chopped green onions
8 oz. Swiss cheese, grated
Dab of butter and/or olive/coconut oil for frying

Lightly beat eggs. Mix flour with milk. Stir in lightly beaten eggs. Add lightly sautéed onion and greens. Over medium heat, melt butter/oil in preheated, non-stick frying pan.
Ladle batter into non-stick pan. Flip when bubbles rise to the top and finish to golden crust. Season pancakes to taste. Then sprinkle 2 heaping tbsp of cheese over each pancake. Serve for breakfast or lunch.

Eating well should be a family affair.

Pesto with Dandegreens

1 cup of firmly packed dandelion leaves, washed, dried and thick lower stems removed
2 ½ tsp. of olive oil
2 ½ tsp. of grated parmesan cheese
1 tsp. of pine nuts
1 ½ cloves of garlic, finely minced
Sea salt to taste

Serve with grilled chicken, pasta, or as a topping for steamed vegetables, or to add flavor for baked tomato slices topped with grated parmesan cheese with dande pesto (bake in oven for 15-20 min at 400°F).
Accompany dandegreen pesto with fish and a slice of lemon.
Enjoy as hors d'oeuvre with dande pesto spread on rye crackers and top with slice of medium cheddar or goat cheese. Enjoy!

During World War II, dandelions were cultivated for the latex extracted from the roots. The latex was used to make rubber.

Dandelions in Batter

2 cups small green, unopened flower (buds) dandelion heads
½ cup of flour
¾ tsp. of sea salt
¼ tsp. of pepper
½ tsp. of baking powder
1 egg, well beaten
½ cup of milk
Olive oil

Gather two cups of blooms, not open, and rinse in cold water. Soak in salt water for about 2 ½ hours.

Prepare egg batter by sifting together flour, sea salt, pepper and baking powder. Blend in egg and milk, and mix well. Dip blossoms into batter, then drop, a few at a time, into olive oil heated to 375°F. Fry until golden brown, turning once.

I served these as hors d'oeuvre or for lunch with cut vegetables. I think they taste like deep fried zucchini.

The roots can be roasted and ground as a coffee substitute.

Dandelion Coffee (single use)

This requires using the root. Wash several times. Water will be muddy, rinse until water is clear. Cut roots into chunks. Rinse again.

Most important step:
Roast chunks on cookie sheet, at 250°F for two hours. Turn roots over. Roast all sides. Roasted root grinds easily using your food processor. Use this powder as you would any type of coffee. You can perk this and by adding other coffee to it, enhances the flavor. This is an excellent way to start your day with a cup of dandelion coffee.

The way it was meant to be for us to use for our own benefit in this now toxic world we live in.

Dandelion Coffee (multiple uses)

To make 32 cups of dandelion coffee, you need 16 cups of undried, unground root.

Clean them and wash several times in a pail of water. Pour off muddy water until such a time that the water is clear.

With a large, sharp knife, cut them into chunks, and wash them again in a clean bowl of water. Pour the water off, add more water, and rinse root until the water is clear.

Grind 2 cups in food processor until you get a mixture of fine and course roots. Repeat with the rest of the roots. Roast on a cookie sheet, a thin layer, @ 250°F for about 2 hours. Stir time to time, roasting on all sides.

In a cup of water, use a tablespoon of root; adjust to your own preference. Or soak root in a coffee pot for 10-15 min

Special thanks to Botanicals.com for their coffee recipes.

One man's weed is another man's livelihood. By Raymond Loo – P.E.I. Potato and Dandelion Farmer.

Dandelion Tea for You

Makes one cup

Pour boiling water in mug or cup over a tea ball filled with 1 tsp. of chopped dried dandelion root. Let stand for a few minutes.
Ingest once, maybe twice a day a few hours apart.
You can make it on the stove in pot of water with equal parts root and boiling water as above, strain serve or cool, put in fridge, good for up to 2 days. Enjoy!
You could possibly enjoy it more by adding an orange slice squeezed into it, or by adding some of juice off your fruit bowls, or add honey or lemon or both.
Side effects your elimination systems and filtering systems are stimulated to clear out. With increased nutrients, your body starts to eliminate better. You get more energy. Win, Win, Situation...

Enjoy a healthy beverage such as dandelion tea to help increase your well-being, one sip at a time.

Dandelion Jelly

4 cups yellow parts of dandelion blossoms
3 cups boiling water
4 ½ cups organic sugar
2 tbsp. freshly squeezed lemon juice
1 pkg. powdered pectin

Pull the yellow blossoms apart from the green parts. Make sure there are no green parts since the green parts may have a bitter flavor. Pack the blossoms into a glass 4 cup measuring cup. More blossoms mean more flavor for the jelly. Bring the water to a boil and fill the water with half of the dandelion blossom heads. Simmer over very gentle heat for about 10 minutes. Pour the water and blossoms through a strainer. Press the blossoms as dry as possible to extract the maximum amount of water. Add more blossoms to the strained water and simmer for about 10 minutes. Continue simmering and straining until all the blossoms are used. Add more water to make 3 cups. You lose some water because it is caught in the blossoms. Strain the water very well. Try though a coffee filter. Combine water with lemon juice, organic sugar and pectin. Bring to a boil and stir until sugar is dissolved and mixture is thickened. Boil hard for one minute. Skim. Pour into hot jars and seal. Add food coloring, if necessary.

Dandelion Uses:
Cosmetic
Culinary
Household
Medicinal

Pumpkin Pie Filling

Pureed pumpkin for one pie (2 cups)
½ cup sugar
1 heaping tsp. of flour
½ tsp. sea salt
1 egg
Nutmeg to taste
⅛ cup milk

Mix first six ingredients together in bowl. Add milk to taste and texture. Put into pie shell. Bake at 425°F for approx. 15 min then turn heat down to 350°F for approx. 1 hr. Cool and decorate at Christmas with Dandelion leaves and raspberries to represent holly and berries.

Grandma Jaynes' recipe.

HOW THE LORD TOLD ME TO CURE CANCER

By George Cairns

(This is a reprint of the article in the Northwest Herald)

Please save this page as it won't be printed again by me. It may save your life or the life of a loved one or a friend. <u>Anyone may reprint this if they print it word for word.</u>

Every week around 10,000 people die of cancer. Government figures show the death rate for cancer deaths has not changed in the last 10 years. Chemo and radiation only save around 10% of the people treated. So this shows our doctors don't have much to work with. As this article goes on I will explain how to prepare this plant and how much to take. There is nothing to buy. For some reason, the Lord has picked me to carry these words to you. I am only the delivery boy, and none of this is my idea. I do believe every word I write here, and I'm a living proof it works. The cost of printing is my thanks to God for giving me back my life and health.

A little over three years ago I was about done in with cancer. One morning as I was waking up and hoping the end would come soon; a voice came to me and said, "You have to do something about your prostate cancer. Take the root of the dandelion. Don't expect a miracle. It took you a long time to get in this condition." The voice was gone. I thought the voice was kidding to use the dandelion. When this voice tells you to do something, you do it. You must do it, like writing this article. It is the last thing I ever expected to do. Then, I thought he didn't tell me how much to take or how to prepare it. As soon as you blink an eye, I knew how much to take, how to prepare it, and it would take 4 to 6 months to cure me. I also knew I wasn't to make a penny on it.

As soon as I got around that morning, I dug some roots and started to prepare it. About a week later I started taking it. Three weeks later the pain in my back and side was gone and my bowels had improved. Five and one half months later they could find no cancer problem in me at all.

I then wanted to find someone else to try it, and that was the biggest problem yet. Nobody seems to want to help. When I told doctors, they just smiled as if I was nuts. Finally, I was telling a friend about it and he said he had a friend that was dying of lung cancer. He had it in both lungs and was bed ridden. They were tapping his lungs. He had been given 4 to 6 weeks to live. After he had been on this powder about six weeks, he was up and around doing his chores and driving his car. He went to his doctor's office, and the doctors could not believe it. They took him to the hospital and gave him a CAT scan. They found no cancer lesions in his lungs and said it was a miracle. I then put an ad in The Northwest Herald offering it free, and found people said they would try it.

Slowly one person told another and it spread. There was a fair amount of people taking in for different kinds of cancer and several for other things. For instance, a man lost the use of his immune system and was told he wouldn't be able to work again for three years, in six months he is now working ½ days and feeling better. I know this is not a cure-all. It won't help everyone or all kinds of cancer. I know it is not a cure for skin cancer and it hasn't had luck with brain tumors. There is a doctor in Boston, Massachusetts that has developed a vaccine that is doing great things. This has been successful with prostate, colon, breast, liver and best of all with lung cancer. Five people have taken it for lung cancer and all five have been cured once. The immune system controls the cancer cells in your body. As long as the immune system is healthy, you don't usually have a cancer problem. When your immune system gets run down it loses control of the cancer cells, and they start eating live cells and this is what they call cancer. This powder made from dandelion root has something in it that builds the blood and the immune system.

When the immune system is built so far, it gets back control of cancer cells, and they do an about face and start cleaning the mess they've made. This is why you must have a fair appetite because your body must build itself and be healthy if you immune system is going to be strong. This will not work for people that have lost their appetite or are on CHEMO. Doctors try to blast the cancer out of your body with Chemo or radiation. By doing so, it destroys your immune system and appetite. These are the most important things your body needs to beat cancer. Operations also knock the immune system haywire. This is why so many people that have operations for cancer find that a short time later it has spread somewhere else.

Many of the worst diseases that have plagued the world have been cured quite easily. When I was a boy, women dreaded the goiter more than cancer. A little iodine in the diet cured that. For hundreds of years the most dreaded diseases was leprosy and lockjaw. A doctor found he could produce penicillin from moldy bread and could cure them and many more things. How long has moldy bread been around? I'm sure scientists will find many uses for the powder made from the root of the dandelions besides cancer. I have already found it builds the blood so you heal much faster.

How to Make It...

To make the powder from the dandelion root you must follow my directions to the letter. Any changes and it won't work. Dig a handful of dandelion roots any time of the year – it doesn't matter. Cut the leaves off just below the crown. DO NOT WASH. Then they must be dried around 100°F. I do it in an incubator with no water. You can also dry them under a heat light bulb, if you raise or lower it so it's 100°F. You can also use the sun or put them in the attic if it's not too hot. It takes about 5 or 6 days in the incubator. I have not done this all the way under the heat light. When you break a root and it snaps it is ready to powder. Take an old iron frying pan and a clean hammer. Take one root at a time and place in the frying pan and start tapping. Don't hit hard or it will fly all over the place. I put my hand around the root to keep most of it in the pan. If it sticks to the hammer and pan, and doesn't crumble in your fingers, it isn't dry enough. Keep it until you have enough to start. It takes about 20 minutes to ½ hour to prepare enough for a week. When you get used to it you can go much faster.

I have an old vessel that druggists used to pound pills (**Mortar & Pestle**), this goes much faster. <u>DO NOT USE AN ELECTRIC GRINDER</u>; it won't work if you do. You lose too much of the good part in dust. You must do it as I have said or don't do it at all. I've tried shortcuts but it seems someone was looking over my shoulder, and I know when I made a mistake. I'm just an old farmer and not a scientist, so I wouldn't know the correct amount to take on my own. Now take a little over one-half teaspoon once a day at any time and mix it with water, orange juice, etc. Do not, use in soft drinks, liquor, or anything hot. When mixed, use it all. Don't let it stand around. Keep the powder in a dry place. After taking it three or four days, you will feel good, but nothing else. That is because your blood is building. When your blood is happy, you're happy. In most cases, this will build your immune system in from three days to three weeks to the point it takes back control of cancer cells and thus the cancer stops spreading. In most cases it is going to help. There is no body feeling as it works. You just feel a little better each week. After three weeks most of the pain will be gone in your back and you know it's working if you had pain there like I did. If you have bone cancer in the spine, it will take three months to work. This is not an overnight cure. It took a while to get in this condition and it will take a while for your body to heal. The sooner you start, the quicker you will be over cancer. Young people heal faster than old people, but will help at any age. I know because I'm 80 years old and have been taking it for over three years. No cancer has come back and no side effects except when my body has had enough, it lets me know by getting heart burn. Then I back off some. Some people get stomach aches when they need less. It also means your cancer is under control and you don't need as much. You will also find you probably won't catch a cold [when] you are taking it full-strength.

The biggest enemy for this root is Chemo. The stronger the Chemo, the less chance the powder has to help you as Chemo tears your immune system and appetite down, two of the most important things you need to cure cancer. There is only a ten percent chance that Chemo will cure you. With no chemo, your chances are 75 to 80% but you must take it every day. Don't let your doctor give you that old trick if you turn him down that goes, "If you want to throw your life away, I can't stop you." Just remember that 90% of the people that take his advice and take chemo are in the cemetery. Don't blame the doctor, he is doing his best with what he has to work with or you could ask for a written guarantee.

I have only mentioned cancers that I know people have had and used this root. It should help pancreas cancer if taken before appetite is gone and most body cancer. This is food, not a drug. It shouldn't interfere with medicine your doctor may be giving you. Only two doctors have told patients to keep taking the powder when they have made a miracle recovery. The rest of the doctors have run the powder down and blasted the people even if the cancer has disappeared.

The medical world is not going to accept this easily.

Going back to not washing the roots and leaving a little soil on them, it is for your own good. A good bit of immunity comes from the soil; it starts as soon as you are born. Your fingers touch something, and you put them in your mouth. A little dirt at first and more as you grow older and start crawling. Then everything you touch goes in the mouth. When children go outside to play and when they come in, they are the dirtiest around the mouth and hand. The hands go in their mouths no matter how dirty they are. Many diseases and bacteria live in the ground, but they don't seem to cause any trouble but it does build the immune system. Some animals can't live if they can't eat a certain amount of soil. If you read this article over, you will see it all goes back to common sense. I wish all of you people with cancer and other problems the best.

George Cairns

Or send self-addressed envelope to: 708 Hughes Road
Woodstock, IL 80096

This article does not necessarily reflect the opinion of the Northwest Herald.
The dandelion root powder you can buy at a Health Food Store is not made the same way. It is not known to help cancer.

Other testimonies

    My friend, Donelda, collects and dry's her dandelion green leaves. She uses them as an herb to sprinkle on her food. It has been leveling out her diabetes to a "normal range" of blood sugar and 50 lbs. of weight loss. Only recently, she was amazed to find out that her pernicious anemia has become leveled out. There is now a less chance of requiring a blood transfusion when levels drop very low. She tried many resources regarding her anemia to which didn't always keep it in a normal range. She has been feeling more energy inside her body. Donelda has said the effects of using dandelions in her food, gives her a positive outlook on her daily health.

    A woman in Maine, U.S.A., whom I met on an anemia support group, has been gravely ill for the last six years. I suggested that she try dandelions in her diet to see if she had any overall improvement in her health. She has recently messaged me to let me know that the dandelion has kept her from having blood transfusions for the last year. Her health was so severe from anemia that she even needed nursing assistance daily. She is now no longer in this debilitating state. Recently, with new renewed health and energy, she is pursuing a lawyer's degree and has the ability of independence of normal everyday living. All thanks to the golden dandelion.

                                           (continued on next page)

An acquaintance of mine is diagnosed with lung cancer and given months to live. He started chemo and radiation therapy and the tumors in both lungs remained. In early Dec. /09, we went to dig dandelions out of the garden. He prepared his collection of roots and greens the same way as George Cairns. After taking ¼ to ½ tsp. twice a day, for six to seven weeks, he went through a period of coughing up phlegm, thinking it might be pneumonia. After continuing the prescription of dandelion until the end of Jan. /10, he then went for another scan of his lungs. There were no lumps in one lung, and one that was reduced from the size of a golf ball, to the size of rice in the other. The doctor said that there was not even enough to biopsy. The doctor then asked what are you doing, and he replied that he was taking dandelion root.

Nearing the end of our conversation, he spoke to me about what has been happening to him these last few weeks, and stated that even the old boy was starting to stand up again in the morning.

Try it for yourself, begin to feel the joy. Share this news with others you care about, so they can feel good too.

Metric Equivalents

1 cup	-	250 ml.
½ cup	-	125 ml.
⅓ cup	-	80 ml.
¼ cup	-	50 ml.
1 tablespoon	-	15 ml.
1 teaspoon	-	5 ml.
½ teaspoon	-	2 ml.
¼ teaspoon	-	1 ml.
2 pounds	-	1 kg.
1 pound	-	0.5 kg.
½ pound	-	0.25 kg.
¼ pound	-	0.125 kg.
1 ounce	-	0 ml (30 g)
1 quart	-	1 L.
1 pint	-	0.5 L.

Suggested sugar conversions:

    Agave syrup
    Maple syrup
    Stevia
    Honey

Bunch   -   Medium to large handful

IT'S A "JOY" PLANT, GRANDMA!

King Kaiden ruled the Kingdom of Kingston. He kept in touch with Princess Sydney from the next castle. She was his sister who ruled Stone Mills. Beween the two family members, they had a goldmine. Dandelion Gold that is.

The people in the kingdom started planting the dandelion seeds in their backyard gardens beside their lettuces, just like their ancestor, Queen Victoria's kingdom did. They would see each year, that a dandelion harvest be organized to collect these herbal plants and they would make sure they use the whole plant. They would make breakfast of fried potatoes and the golden yellow flowers for children and families at the local schools. They would also collect the green leaves for use in recipes from their Nanny's Green Cookbook called "Living Dande``.

They all learned to preserve, dry and or freeze, the rest of the dandelion for later use. The root, they would dry for tea or roast for coffee, or crush it for a cure for sickness. I tell you they were brilliant!

They saved their Kingdom and the world from a lot of disease and starvation by doing this. They also did a collection of the flowers once they'd gone to seed, to send out to missions in other countries so they too, could grow and reap the benefits of this Golden Green plant, too.

You know they saved a lot of lives by getting this knowledge out. No more major health problems for the people of this world, because everybody got information about proper nutrition.

People just felt good and by everyone working together, they created a joyous environment, and everyone, everywhere lived happily ever after.

Original story by Debbie Richmond.

The green, honest to God debate.

About the Author

My name is Deborah Louise Jaynes Richmond. However, my friends call me Debbie or Deb. Dandelions and I had a life time of mutual admiration. As a child my first great love was gathering bouquets of dandelions which I used to decorate anything I could find, such as my sand box cakes, my toys, my hair, then offering my sunny gifts of bouquets to my mother.

Growing up in a small hamlet, such as Yarker (Simcoe Falls), it is here that following my Fathers and Mothers examples, I learned to work, and volunteer in my community. My own peer group knew the security of having the most wonderful friends and neighbors.

After completing high school, I earned my RPN at St. Lawrence College in Kingston. Over the years, working at this profession, brought me great personal satisfaction. My husband Kevin, and my two children, Kiel and Megan, were very supportive.

Tragic events that changed my life

All of you have probably heard of any story of being rear ended in a car accident. The truth is this incident did a great deal of internal damage to my abdominal, pelvic, shoulder-neck and even my teeth cracked and I required fillings. Chronic pain consumed my body, my mind, and all of my waking and sleeping hours. Realizing that my body had become so toxic, fibromyalgia and chronic pain set in, as well as psoriasis with a vengeance. Discovery was near. I studied Natural Nutrition, Aging Body, Aging Mind, and received a doctorate of natural medicine from EBNMP™. In my own home, I began to practice ion cleansing a detoxifying foot bath. I tell people that this is like an oil change on your body. This is also an extension of my holistic medicine practice.

How I changed my mind about wellness

Imagine that my first love of dandelions would play such an important part in my road to recovery. This started for me in the year 2002. Now, the question I ask myself is, "Can I teach other people who read this book, that dandelions are such an important part of nature, and can HEAL." Now I feel it is my mission in life, to educate as much as I can. This is the purpose of this book.

Debbie Richmond
P.S.: I want to let people know that I've finally returned to work as a nurse. There is a light at the end of the tunnel after this healing crisis.

My Vision;

-Is to see millions of people using wisdom of the past to stay Healthy & well, by picking dandelion seeds and sending them in envelopes to specified collection drop offs. Then have them sent to places to be planted, for use as food or medicine anywhere in the world that they are needed. Do you know how good a dandelion might look to someone who is starving, or only has one choice of food in his bowl? A dandelions high nutrient count might also look good to someone who wants their body to work better.

I think there are more than enough dandelions and men women & children who could help. Heck, why stop with just collecting seed, why not collect the whole plant and put it to everyone's good use. Then we all could all be Living Dande!

For further information, contact me in writing, with a self addressed stamped envelope at;

R.R. 2, Yarker, Ontario, Canada.
K0K 3N0

CPSIA information can be obtained
at www.ICGtesting.com
Printed in the USA
BVHW030528140821
614143BV00001B/76